PRAISE FOR *A LONG WALK DOWN A WINDING ROAD*

"This book will be a welcome read for families looking for insight into how the future can be brighter and how important family, the right diagnosis, and appropriate supports can be in making this happen."

—Barbara Gantwerk, former New Jersey state director of special education

"Too often society suggests that individuals have reached their fullest potential as young adults; they are labeled as either abled or disabled. Farmer provides a fresh outlook to positively persuade us from this negative mindset. His unique and personal insight into neurodiversity is proof that social and emotional growth are a lifelong journey. Through honest reflection (and a splash of humor), he recognizes the importance family, peers, therapists, and employers have had on his life and shares the strategies he's applied toward becoming more socially aware. *A Long Walk Down a Winding Road* is a brilliant and personal illustration of self-growth, love, and acceptance."

—Lucy Ann Johnson, executive director, Transitions Life Center & Community: A Special Place for Special Needs

"By interspersing his memoir with helpful how-to advice, Sam has created a resource as valuable to someone on the spectrum as it is to the clinicians who serve them. His distinct voice and meticulous inner dialogue allow the reader to take his perspective in situations as diverse as the workplace, love, and family relationships and to realize that the difference in experience of 'Aspies' versus 'neurotypicals' is less than you'd think."

—Kim Lewis, M.Ed CCC-SLP, speech-language pathologist, Activity Tailor

"*A Long Walk Down a Winding Road* is an inspirational and worthwhile read. Sam writes with purpose and sincerity as he shares his experiences, challenges, and insights. We all can learn from Sam's example and his transformative life lessons."

—Karen, speech language pathologist

"Sam Farmer reaches into his past, evaluates his present, and starts paying his experiences forward after an in-depth description of his journey through being diagnosed with Asperger's syndrome. He takes you down a fascinating path of how he interprets the world around him and how he's learned to be a part of it."

—Michelle L. Carney, M.Ed, BCBA, LBA, master ABA program consultant, Autism Outreach / Club ED

"Sam's honest reflection of his life will resonate with adults on the autism spectrum, especially those who discovered their diagnosis later in life as he did. Drawing from his experiences as a child, a husband,

and a father of an autistic son, his book will provide the reader with practical suggestions and insight into how someone on the autism spectrum can navigate the world and build a fulfilling life."

—Dania Jekel, executive director, the Asperger/Autism Network

"In his beautifully written book, *A Long Walk Down a Winding Road,* Farmer conveys hopefulness and optimism about the possibilities for individuals with Asperger's or autism spectrum disorder. His journey toward self-knowledge and his advice on how he overcame and still struggles with some obstacles will let others in the Aspie community know they are not alone in their experiences. His story informs clinicians too. Hearing how well Farmer has done gives me, and hopefully others, inspiration to stay in the field and keep helping."

—Nancy K. Gajee, PhD, director of outpatient clinical services, Judge Baker Children's Center, Boston

A LONG WALK DOWN A WINDING ROAD

A LONG WALK DOWN A WINDING ROAD

SMALL STEPS, CHALLENGES, & TRIUMPHS THROUGH AN AUTISTIC LENS

SAM FARMER

FOREWORD BY ***Nancy Clements, MA, CCC-SLP***

Published by Spectrum Wisdom Publishing, Easton, MA,
Samfarmerauthor.com

Edited and designed by Girl Friday Productions
www.girlfridayproductions.com

Cover design: Anna Curtis
Project management: Bethany Davis
Image credits: cover © Shutterstock / ExpediTom

ISBN (paperback): 978-1-7333723-0-5
ISBN (e-book): 978-1-7333723-1-2
Library of Congress Control Number: 2019911828

First edition

In memory of Mom and Dad

FOREWORD

What does it mean to grow up with a condition and not know it? What happens when you discover the condition at forty years of age? Does it become an excuse for a lifetime of missteps and confusion? Or does it lead to a journey of understanding who you are and a burning desire to help others understand themselves?

Asperger's syndrome as a diagnosis no longer exists in the *Diagnostic and Statistical Manual of Mental Disorders* (*DSM*), but it still is widely used to represent a culture and community of individuals that brings to the world a specific profile of learning strengths and vulnerabilities (like all of us). Those who have been diagnosed with Asperger's have a strong IQ and specific talents. They also share challenges with social communication and struggle with the specific processes associated with social competence. These challenges can also result in increased anxiety and depression.

In the chapters that follow, Sam leads us all on his lifetime journey of understanding himself as a person who loves music; is kind, sensitive, and deeply convicted in his beliefs; and has Asperger's syndrome. With a late diagnosis, he describes his lifetime of joys and struggles through the lens of knowing he was a "stranger in a strange land" and learning to embrace himself as a son, student, friend, professional, husband, and father. He allows us glimpses into the profound wisdom of his mother, who, as a social worker, set the stage of accepting Sam's functioning and learning within a neurodiverse world from an early age. His resulting tenacity and grit are highlighted as essential in overcoming setbacks and celebrating triumphs.

I invite you to share Sam's adventures, reflections, and insights. His story offers advice and inspiration to parents, educators, and individuals. Throughout the development of this book, I have advocated for this combination of memoir and self-help, which contains golden nuggets of humanity and acceptance that should be embraced by all of us!

Nancy Clements, MA, CCC-SLP
Sam's Social Coach
Executive Director, Social Thinking Boston

INTRODUCTION

THE PAYING-IT-FORWARD MISSION

When I think about the word "luck," I imagine an ideal world in which all who are good-natured and deserving would have enough of it to live happy, fulfilling lives. For some time now, I have considered myself to be extraordinarily lucky, for all that I have and all that I have been given. At the same time, I know that too many others are equally if not more entitled to luck yet are not as fortunate. Not everything in life is fair, and good fortune is not evenly or equitably distributed. Though maybe, just maybe, I can do something to help.

My name is Sam Farmer. Husband, father, computer consultant, musician, and owner of an autism spectrum profile are among the many hats that I wear. Perhaps you are surprised that I feel as lucky as I do, given the autism diagnosis. But with time, hard work, and an optimistic attitude, I have learned to embrace it, and I am not the only one on the spectrum who can tell this kind of story. My particular story—my journey toward self-acceptance, success, happiness, setbacks, adversity, and triumphs, including what I have learned along the way and the people who have played significant roles in my narrative—is embodied in this book.

The extent to which the people in my life have helped shape the person I am today is truly extraordinary to me. So many of the folks with whom I have had significant relationships were invaluable to the equation: I would not be as emotionally strong or socially competent as I have become, my work ethic would not be what it is, my self-esteem might be in the gutter, and I would have no knowledge of my autism spectrum profile without even one of them. Not that I am giving all of the credit to other people; doing so would be selling myself short, given all of my efforts toward personal growth. Nonetheless, their influence is undeniable.

I am referring to my wife, son, mother, father, and brothers; several therapists and clinicians with whom I have worked over the years; friends; former and current co-workers; folks with whom I have studied and performed music; the directors of the special-needs summer camps I attended when I was growing up; and many exceptional teachers who opened my eyes to a world of knowledge and helped bring to fruition all of the potential they saw in me. The long walk down the winding road that characterizes my life has been greatly facilitated by all of them.

As for the winding road on which I continue to walk, I see it in three phases: partially informed, enlightened, and, now, paying it forward. My mother got the whole process started back when I was a little shy of three years old, at which time she noticed that something was amiss with respect to my awareness of the surroundings and my ability to gather and process information from the immediate environment. She once admitted to me that she could see it in the blue of my eyes; she would be speaking to me and noticed that I was staring back at her, blank-faced, often with no physical or verbal response to what she was saying, as if her words were passing through me with little or no absorption. Thankfully, she realized that she needed to take action as soon as she noticed this. She insisted on finding an explanation for her observations and the proper help for me so that we could begin to tackle these issues sooner rather than later. Her initial efforts soon led us to a learning specialist and a diagnosis of a learning disability in auditory perception.

When my learning disability was discovered in the early 1970s, autism was not thought of as a spectrum disorder as it is today. At the time, only those profiles on the more extreme end of the spectrum were considered to be indicative of autism. My profile was not considered extreme. As such, "learning-disabled" was the sole diagnosis. Back then, my family and I had identified one member of our neighborhood as being autistic by virtue of the severity of his challenges as well as his unique abilities. He had a particularly difficult time making direct eye contact and more often than not would exhibit his remarkable talent for memorizing and reciting personal information about me or people close to me (our exact addresses, ages, birth dates, phone numbers, etc.), which I was shocked that he knew because we were not friends and one or more years would typically go by between interactions.

My youthful challenges, which involved information processing and connectivity to what was going on around me, resulted in my missing many verbal and nonverbal cues from others, a frequent appearance of disinterest in other people's lives, self-absorption, and a tendency to unintentionally say irrelevant, uninformed, insensitive, and sometimes hurtful things to people who mattered to me. Case in point: when I was thirteen, my family made a trip to Israel during which we spent a good chunk of our time driving across the country with our tour guide in his car. One day, as we were driving through a region of some significance (I can't recall exactly where), the only question that occurred to me to ask him was "How many miles per gallon does your car get?" Never mind that he was sharing interesting information about the region's history and culture. How's that for being engaged in the here and now! My question never got answered.

Because there were significant differences between my profile and that of my neighbor, my diagnosis was relegated to that of a learning disability and nothing more. The "partially informed" phase of my life had taken hold in that I knew of my learning disability but not my autism profile. In retrospect, better one than none! I am fortunate that the learning disability was detected early on, and that I had a mother who was passionate about helping me, arranging therapies and special schooling and lots more, without stalling or making excuses for inaction.

Fast-forward to age forty. At the time, I had been married for nine years, had a one-year-old son, and carried many of the same challenges I had while growing up, though thankfully at significantly diminished levels of intensity. My wife had been wondering for some time if there was more going on with me than just a learning disability, granted all of the challenges that we were confronting as a married couple (more on this later). In light of my newfound role as a father and my acknowledgment of the depth of responsibility and importance that is associated with this role, somehow I finally felt compelled to listen to her and sought help in learning more about myself. I found a local therapist whom I eventually asked, in so many words, "Is there a test or an evaluation I can undergo that would help me determine whether there is another diagnosis besides my learning disability?" After considering my question and all that she had learned about me during our sessions, the therapist ended up recommending a neuropsychological evaluation. Understanding what might be at stake if I chose not to be evaluated, I decided to proceed.

After enduring a full day of tiring and intensive testing and waiting a month or two for the report, the missing puzzle piece emerged. "Asperger's syndrome," the neuropsychologist's report concluded, which I understood at the time to be a higher-functioning form of autism. It was as if the words jumped off the page at light speed and smacked me in the face! I felt not only regretful but also blindsided and confused. Regretful because I wished that I had known years earlier, prior to marrying and becoming a father. Blindsided because I did not see this revelation coming. And confused because I was well acquainted with somebody diagnosed with Asperger's; I vividly remembered the autistic neighbor from my childhood years; and I had a difficult time reconciling what I knew about these two people with what I had just learned about myself. The diagnosis would ultimately be validated by every one of the several clinicians I ended up working with in my efforts to manage my newly discovered Aspie (a more upbeat way of saying "Asperger's") profile.

Before long, regret and confusion gave way to clarity, and finally, the emergence of an explanation for a lifetime of struggle that, for the most part, had been due to social competence–related difficulties. As my post-Aspie-diagnosis work with clinicians progressed, I started to learn about what Asperger's syndrome entails. Gradually, many lingering questions from my childhood and early adulthood, questions that my learning disability diagnosis never properly answered, were now starting to be addressed. Why was it often an overwhelming chore to meet people and make friends? Why had I kept striking out with girls? What accounted for all of the bullying I endured? How could I have a learning disability, considering that I had amassed plenty of knowledge and always performed well in school? Why were my greatest challenges in social situations outside the classroom? A thorough education about my newfound diagnosis filled in all of these blanks and then some, and it was at that point that I finally began to transition from the "partially informed" phase of my life to the "enlightened" phase.

Soon after I was finally granted a complete picture of the person looking back at me in the mirror, it dawned on me how truly remarkable it was that all of the right people came into my life at the perfect time, in the perfect order, and with the right ideas and methods to provide the help I needed. What if it had not occurred to my wife that there might be more going on with me than my learning disability? What if the therapist had no legitimate reason to recommend a neuropsychological evaluation? What if the neuropsychologist failed to conclude that I had Asperger's syndrome? Even though it wasn't until I was forty years old that I uncovered a significant aspect of my personality, I am quite fortunate that all of the pieces fell into place the way they did. Better late than never!

Regrettably, many folks on the autism spectrum never make this discovery, or find out much later in life than I did, and as a result, either end up without access to or must wait for the professional assistance that they deserve and from which I have greatly benefited. Furthermore, many are left to wonder why they must contend with challenges that are alien to most other people, challenges that stem from being autistic in a world that is shaped by the nonautistic majority. My views on how those of us on the autism spectrum must try to succeed amid social and behavioral expectations created by those without autism are not in any way meant to be divisive or suggestive of an "us versus them" dynamic. At the end of the day, we all share a common humanity that unites us, and, as is the case with plenty of Aspies, I have friends, family, and acquaintances without autism who are very close and important to me. Furthermore, as this book will illustrate, some of my challenges are also the challenges of others not on the spectrum. Rather, I have come to believe that an Asperger's diagnosis is a diagnosis not for a disorder but instead for a *different* way of looking at the world, of thinking and learning about it, of processing information and reacting to it. To me, the term "autism spectrum" should therefore not be referred to as a disorder but instead as a unique set of cognitive and behavioral traits resulting from an alternative neurology, and which warrant special interventions, clinical treatments, and therapies to help with challenges that arise from being autistic in an essentially neurotypical (nonautistic) world. If you think that I am trying to have my cake and eat it too by saying that autism is not truly a disorder yet is deserving of these types of accommodations, that's fine, I get it! Then again, who says that one must have a disorder to be worthy of assistance?

In spite of the above, I use the words "disability," "disorder," and "diagnosis" throughout this book because they are familiar and are often included in writing or discussion of the autism spectrum. That said, my wish is that they not be interpreted at face value. The optimist in me chooses not to look at my Aspie profile in these terms because doing so would be counterproductive and would likely compromise my sense of self. Rather, I look at Asperger's as being at the core of who I am as a person.

My oldest brother recently echoed this sentiment when we were talking on the phone. He said, "You know, Sam, I understand that you were diagnosed with Asperger's, but the family always thought of you simply as Sam." I replied, in so many words, "Yes, absolutely. I am still the same person that you have always known, though I have come to embrace Asperger's as being central to who I am."

Many have asked if there will ever be a cure for autism. In the event that one is developed at some point in the future, I would outright reject it without hesitation. How much of my personality would be irretrievably lost? Who would I be? I would likely become unrecognizable to myself.

As I mentioned earlier, my mom was the first to begin to understand my challenges and to track down the appropriate help. She passionately continued to guide me in every way that she could throughout my youth and into adulthood, and her efforts phenomenally paid off. Her death in 2016 transformed me in more ways than one. For starters, I developed the courage to reveal my autism spectrum diagnosis to people outside my immediate family (whom I told shortly after being diagnosed in 2009), and I did so while eulogizing her at her funeral, to give meaning and context to all that she did to help me move forward. Since then, it has become easy for me to open up about my Aspie profile, when appropriate, to anybody. My transformation also involved a level of social awareness that I had seldom exhibited beforehand; it occurred to me to think about how to word my eulogy and my "coming out" in a way that would not draw too much attention to myself. It also occurred to me to talk about my Aspie profile in a way that would be sensitive to the feelings of those in attendance who were on the autism spectrum or had a family member on the spectrum. Clearly, the funeral and my eulogy had to center around my mother, not around me, and thankfully, that is how it was received.

The final paragraph in the eulogy reads: "Mom, wherever you may be, if you can hear me, I will always be eternally grateful for all that you gave me and did for me. To me, you were more than just a loving, caring, nurturing mother. In fact, you were nothing less than a transformative force in my life, and I may not be the only one here today whose life you transformed. I love you, I miss you, and I thank you, from the bottom of my heart."

The eulogy was received warmly and carried enough emotional impact such that a few of the people who heard it urged me to write it down and publish it. Once on paper, I shared it with my speech language pathologist (SLP), with whom I had been working extensively for a few years on enhancing social competence. She referred me to the executive director of the Asperger/Autism Network (AANE), who agreed that my tribute was worthy of being posted on the website's blog (www.aane.org/blog). And so, "A Spectrum Son's Tribute to His Mom" was published in 2016. It was at that point that the current phase of my life up to now was underway, that of "paying it forward."

Once my mother passed on, I could no longer pay her back for all of her efforts, so I decided instead to pay it forward, and to do so in her memory. When my father passed away not long thereafter, I became that much more passionate about my "paying-it-forward mission," now being carried out to honor their collective legacy. I choose to pay it forward by sharing ideas and insight as to how one can find success and happiness in spite of the challenges and adversity that come with an Asperger's or autism spectrum diagnosis. I do so with the hope that those I reach will be able to carve out better lives for themselves.

The paying-it-forward mission started with the posting of my tribute to my mother on the AANE blog. It continues with additional blogs and articles that are posted on an ongoing basis on the same and other websites, as well as coaching videos, presentations at conferences, involvement with community support groups, and this book. I intend to keep at it indefinitely, for as long as I am able. If one or more of the ideas that I share can have a positive impact on the lives of others, then I will feel as though I have succeeded.

So it is that I write this book, in part for my own benefit, because I have found writing to be therapeutic and helpful in my efforts to address personal challenges that stem from my profile. However, this book is not merely an exercise in me helping myself by writing a memoir; it is also a guide with ideas that I have picked up over the course of my life, which I believe may be of value not merely to folks in the autism spectrum community, but to others as well. First and foremost, I write with others in mind, and it is my sincere hope that every reader will benefit from or be inspired by at least a portion of what I have to say. I am keeping my fingers crossed that it will do just that, that it will make a positive difference in your life or in the life of somebody whom you teach, work with, care for, or love. Perhaps its use will lead to outcomes similar to mine, even if the beneficiary has not been as lucky as I feel I have been. Significant personal change requires considerably more than luck, as is evidenced in this book. Hard work, patience, perseverance, and help from others are also essential to improved outcomes.

Lastly, I learned a long time ago that brevity is a virtue, that "less is often more," and so I am deliberately keeping this book relatively short to make it more accessible to the reader. With that said, if there is a topic raised in the book that you'd like to know more about, please find me at samfarmerauthor.com and let me know. I will respond as soon as I am able.

All the best,

Sam Farmer

CHAPTER 1

MOM, DAD, AND MY FORMATIVE YEARS

Simply put, my objective in life has always been to be happy and successful in whatever I do. I feel as though I have attained that goal largely because of my parents' efforts, from the beginning, at helping me move forward. How my parents, Maxine and Steve Farmer, helped me move forward contributed to the kind of person I have become: resilient, wise, hardworking, optimistic, and good at heart.

My mother, as a social worker; my father, as a doctor; and both of them, as loving parents and as loyal friends, gave so much of themselves to others and instilled this value in me and in my brothers. They both taught us, by example, that you get what you give in this life and that it is important to make a positive difference.

Shortly after my mother passed away, following a long battle with dementia, one of her dearest friends said all that needed to be said in just a few words: "Sam, there could not have been a better mother in the world for you than your mom." It takes a guiding hand that is strong, intelligent, loving, and unwavering to effectively help somebody through the kinds of challenges and struggles that I have faced, and that kind of guiding hand, without question, belonged to my mother. Several aspects of her personality and parenting style account for why she contributed to my long-term success and happiness more than anybody else. She laid the foundation on which I was able to build a life for myself while also helping me through that building process.

My mother's unsurpassed abilities at connecting with and understanding other people were of critical importance to me from the start. Her background as a psychology major and social worker had much to do with these talents. To this day, I remain in awe of how she managed to figure out on her own, and in the early 1970s, that I had special needs and challenges when I was only two years old. It was my great fortune to have a mother who understood the urgency of taking immediate action once she figured out what she did and who wholeheartedly committed herself to a mission from which nothing in the world could distract her. Quickly tracking down a capable learning specialist and the subsequent learning disability diagnosis were just the beginning. Once I reached kindergarten, my mom discovered that the school district in my hometown of Princeton, New Jersey, had not yet established a special education program, and so she found an out-of-district elementary school for special-needs kids for me to attend. By second grade, I was ready to be "mainstreamed" into a general education classroom while also spending time in the special education program that my hometown school district introduced that year. By fifth grade, I was ready to transition out of special education and into the general education classroom full-time. Hard work, good teachers, lots of guidance from my mother around how I could compensate for my learning difficulties, my mother's advocacy efforts in the schools, an extra year (I was held back either after kindergarten or first grade; I cannot remember which), and plenty of encouragement from both of my parents enabled me to make these strides.

English, particularly reading comprehension, was my greatest academic challenge during my primary school years and thereafter. In retrospect, it made perfect sense that I struggled with this subject, considering that my learning disability is one of auditory perception, and given my Aspie profile. My difficulties around processing information from my surroundings and the resultant disconnect from others that I often felt logically had an adverse effect on how I comprehended themes, main ideas, and the characters in stories and books. My mother understood all of this very well and made sure that I received plenty of help in this area. Her efforts paid off, as was evidenced by how well I managed to do in fifth grade with a teacher who, as I'll never forget, greatly emphasized reading books and writing reports about them over every other subject. My mother never told me outright, but it would not surprise me if she had something to do with my placement with this teacher, knowing in advance that my reading comprehension and writing skills would improve while in her classroom. She probably did.

My mother's devotion to my advancement was not only with respect to my education. Starting at age ten, I was sent to sleepaway camps that offered developmental opportunities for kids with special needs for two months or so each summer. By the time I turned fifteen, I had outgrown that type of experience and was ready for camps intended for neurotypical kids, which I continued to attend through the summer after my junior year of high school. Spending time away from home and my family each year helped instill in me a strong sense of independence, which would prove invaluable as I worked to address my challenges. I discovered many new pursuits that otherwise would have eluded me and was able to cultivate existing interests; chief among these was music. It was at summer camp that I met my first girlfriend, learned how to water-ski, felt well liked by most of my peers for the first time in my life, first performed with an orchestra and a jazz band, and, during the summer of 1987, was formally recognized as an honor camper. I enjoyed levels of freedom that simply were not possible during the school year, including being given the latitude to decide for myself which activities to pursue and how much time I would devote to them, when and for how long I would practice piano, when and if I felt like eating breakfast, lunch, and dinner, et cetera.

Consequently, my self-esteem was helped at a critical time in my life when I was contending with self-esteem-compromising challenges around self-absorption and social unawareness.

My mother's efforts to set me up for success continued when she chose private school for my middle and high school years. Smaller class sizes, the availability of after-school extra help, and a highly regarded perceptual training program for students with unique challenges made a tremendous difference with respect to academic achievement. Furthermore, there was a well-enforced honor code in place, which kept most of us relatively well behaved. Not once did I get bullied throughout my seven years at this school, despite my social competency–related deficits, thanks not only to the honor code but also to the kinds of people with whom I was most fortunate to share my secondary school years. I keep in touch with many of my classmates to this day, a true testament to the unbreakable bond we felt as a class, one that has persisted for thirty-plus years.

Not every mother knows where to draw the line between constructive and destructive criticism, but my mom knew. She understood that I was hypersensitive when it came to being judged, corrected, or reprimanded. She knew when to bite her tongue, which battles were or were not worth fighting, when to let go, and when to allow me to learn from my own mistakes, in my own way, and in my own time. She put in place a culture within our family whereby my father and brothers learned to treat me as she did. Antisocial behaviors and missed social cues that she felt I could not control were, for the most part, not called out. She had a strong sense of humor, an integral part of her parenting style that created a safe and inviting atmosphere in which I could be myself without negative consequence. My quirky or idiosyncratic habits were never ridiculed, only subject to what could be called "safe teasing," whereby my brothers and parents would laugh with me rather than at me and imitate these habits as a way of showing that I was accepted by them for who I was. It was all about preserving my self-esteem, which, due to the baggage connected to my learning disability (and undiagnosed Aspie profile), was quite fragile.

My mom's protective instincts resulted in my not being disciplined for what many would consider a number of discipline-worthy incidences. I remember a family trip to the beach one summer when I turned her in to the beach-house attendant after she admitted to bending one of the rules (I cannot remember which one—it wasn't as if the crime of the century had been committed), and I heard not a word from her about it. On parents' visiting day at sleepaway camp one year, she gave me an enthusiastic hello and a big smile, followed by my saying to her, verbatim, "You've gained weight!" No rebuke from her or my dad, and the remainder of the day proceeded well, as if I had never said what I had. In fifth grade, the highly anticipated day arrived for my interview with the dean of admissions at the private middle school that my mom was so eager to have me attend, and I said, in my often brutally honest tone, "I don't want to go here; I don't like it here," or something along those lines. I will never be able to explain what led to my gutter attitude that day. I can only assume that I felt I had better things to do, or that I was in a bad mood for some reason and could not keep it to myself. Yet again, my mother did not discipline me; although years later, when we were reminiscing about this incident, she admitted that I nearly gave her a heart attack. What I would give to know what she said to the dean of admissions that resulted in my acceptance, in spite of my obnoxious comments. In most cases, I'm sure that this kind of behavior would at least be called out, if not harshly punished, but she knew me well and was wise enough to understand that doing so would have been more destructive than constructive. For that kind of wisdom, I will always be grateful to her.

My mom was exceptional at striking a balance between hands-on and hands-off parenting. She understood the importance of compromise, of give-and-take, and of allowing me to make decisions but not without considering the potential consequences beforehand. If kids in the neighborhood were outside playing and I was inside, I heard about it from her and was strongly encouraged to participate; however, I was allowed to opt out if I so desired. As far as the special-needs summer camps were concerned, she chose these camps but left it up to me to decide how many summers I would go to each one. Starting in the summer after my eighth-grade year, she allowed me to choose where I would go.

During my later high school years, when my passion for music peaked, I told myself that I would leave my high school and attend an arts academy for senior year, and I became convinced that I belonged at a music school as far as college was concerned. Thankfully, my mom got through to me and brought me back down to earth, not by telling me to forget about it or by putting the matter to rest some other way but instead by encouraging me to think carefully about these choices before making a decision. She asked me to consider how I would feel leaving my friends and the school I had been at and loved for six years just before graduating. She also stressed the importance of a well-rounded, liberal arts–based college education versus one that focused more heavily on music performance, reminding me that I could still major in music wherever I went. Knowing deep down that she knew what she was talking about, and respecting her opinions on these matters, I chose to listen to her. I remained where I belonged for my senior year, attended a highly rated liberal arts college with an elite music school, and graduated with the degree in music that I always wanted. While a music major, I also studied the wide variety of other subjects in which I became interested while in college, all with no regrets. And so it was from my mother that I learned the importance of surrounding myself with smart, caring people and taking their advice and wisdom to heart.

She knew me better than I knew myself during these formative years. She understood my strengths and vulnerabilities and tailored her parenting style accordingly. In hindsight, I find it remarkable that I was allowed to make as many of my own choices as I did, considering all of my challenges. Evidently, she knew that the way forward for me required that I be given enough latitude to find my own path with some but not too much oversight. Only when it mattered most, when the stakes were relatively high, or when I turned to her for support, did she get involved, and she did so with love and conviction, in a way that somehow achieved the proper result far more often than not. Granted what I was up against while growing up, there truly could not have been a better mother in the world for me than my mom.

As had been the case with my mom's passing, my dad's was also the end result of a hard-fought battle with dementia, one that thankfully ended peacefully, in his own home, and in the midst of people who cared about him. Unlike my mom's passing, I was actually there when my dad passed on, and, for the first time in my life, I felt the kind of emptiness that can only be felt once both parents have departed. The combination of bearing witness and, at the same time, realizing that my brothers and I now represented the elder generation in the immediate family was profound to me but not emotionally overwhelming. When he was healthy, my father made it clear more than once that he did not want me or anybody else to cry over him when his day came, and he hoped that everybody would simply continue to live their lives as if nothing had happened. So that's what I did, for the most part. Though tears were shed from time to time, both for him and for my mother, I have remained mostly stoic, which has helped me cope with my loss. Emotional stoicism is a common attribute among folks on the autism spectrum, whereby we tend not to display our feelings, and I am no exception. It does not mean that I am emotionless—though sadly, for many on the spectrum, it is often misconstrued as such, leading to many of us being misunderstood. It only means that some of us deal with our feelings in a way that keeps them below the surface, though these feelings are no less real than those of people who are more expressive.

My father was a relatively laid-back, "go with the flow" type of person, with a big heart and nerves of steel; it was difficult to get under his skin and anger him. That worked out well for me as I was growing up, considering how sensitive I was to confrontation, criticism, and getting yelled at. He got me started with tennis, cross-country running, and music, knowing that I would be successful at these pursuits and that they would therefore contribute to my happiness and self-esteem. However, it was his emphasis on the importance of hard work, of taking pride in work and doing it well, that had the greatest impact on me. He taught this by example. As a doctor of roughly fifty years, in practice until he was almost eighty years young, the degree to which he helped other people is immeasurable. The remarkable number of patients he took care of and the outcomes he achieved for them were testaments to his commitment to excellence and the passion he felt for his work. The extra time and effort he invested in the folks under his care was admirable and earned him great respect in the Princeton medical community and across the town. This was how he operated on a daily basis, regardless of how busy he was, and without exception.

If he delegated tasks to me and my brothers and we did them halfway, he'd let us know about it. Whenever he told me to clean the fish tank in his office, I therefore took it upon myself to make sure that the glass sides were no less than 100 percent free of green algae. I had to painstakingly scrape it all off, from top to bottom, inch by inch, around the entire perimeter of the tank. Somebody had to do this work; it might as well have been me. Once done, he would often say to me, "Great job. Now doesn't it feel good knowing that you did the job right?"

I fondly remember the road trips my father and I took to visit my aunt, uncle, and grandparents once I earned my driver's license and was the one to drive both ways. He always had a phenomenal amount of paperwork to get through and often needed to find creative ways to get it done. He couldn't do it while driving, so he would work in the back seat of the car while I drove. I marveled at that and admired his willpower, considering that he managed to complete a good amount of it despite how tall he was, sitting in the back seat of our not-all-that-big car while dealing with frequent bumps in the road and also having occasional conversations with me along the way.

Once my brothers and I had families of our own, we would sometimes take vacations together, renting out large houses. Often, we'd find our father with patient files and other medical paperwork strewn across the dining room table, as if it had become his oversized desk. I was never put off by him choosing to work over the course of a family get-together. Being a doctor was core to his identity, as was the devotion he felt for his chosen profession. Besides, he never spent *all* of our vacation time in this fashion, and it was enough for us that we were all under one roof doing our own things.

My father's passion for his work was applauded by my mother, particularly when his birthday came around during his older years. She would often tell me that the best gift he received on his birthday, and a blessing granted his age, was simply being able to go to the office, take care of his patients, and come home, satisfied, having put in a good day's work. I agreed with her. It was all about mind over matter and loving what you do.

What must an Aspie with a learning disability do to succeed academically? Commit to doing well—no half measures! What must an Aspie possess to acquire social skills and cultivate meaningful and lasting friendships? Stick-to-itiveness! What does an Aspie need if he or she chooses to either significantly diminish or conquer aspects of his or her profile to live a better life? A relentless work ethic! My father taught me all about these important character traits and behaviors simply by being who he was.

And so my walk down this winding road continues, and I know I will never be alone as I move forward. My memories of my parents will remain with me, keeping me strong and inspiring me to greater things. As a parent myself, I endeavor to take the best aspects of my mother's and father's parenting styles and incorporate them into my own. Easier said than done! Together, they are one tough act to follow.

CHAPTER 2

ADVENTURES IN DEVELOPING SOCIAL COMPETENCE

If only I knew then what I know now! Most of us have probably said that to ourselves at least once when looking back and wondering what might have been. What if we had done something a little differently, stepped out of our comfort zone instead of resorting to the path of least resistance, or chosen to walk the walk rather than talk the talk? There is no going back, though we can certainly draw lessons from the past to move forward into the future more intelligently.

While growing up and into early adulthood, I knew little about socialization; thankfully, I have been able to learn a great deal from past mistakes as I work to develop social competencies. Moving forward in this regard has required small steps over many years, with occasional regressions and many sometimes-painful lessons learned the hard way. That's the nature of the beast when it comes to my autism spectrum profile. Unlike neurotypical people, who seem to naturally possess varying degrees of social awareness, I had to learn social skills and awareness from scratch. As a result, my younger years were characterized by a level of social competence that was not on par with that of most other kids my age, making it particularly challenging for me to cultivate friendships. I simply needed more time to grow up as well as support from those who were in a position to help me learn what most of my peers already knew.

I am a good person at heart, friendly, well intentioned, polite, patient, and loyal to those who matter to me. I have always tried to see the best in others and to do right by them. I follow through on my promises as best I can and refrain from prejudice, forming opinions about people based only on their character and how they treat me and other people. Qualities such as these have made it possible for me to make friends with those who saw value in my personality and were willing and able to look past my social skills challenges. Thanks largely to them, I gradually improved at establishing meaningful, lasting friendships, and my social skills, self-awareness, and awareness of others improved as a result. Today, I am a husband of almost nineteen years, a father of eleven years, and I have friends who have been in it with me for the long haul, a few since grade-school days.

Despite all that I have going for me, I can never stop focusing on personal growth and learning because many of those same childhood challenges persist to this day and must continue to be addressed as my roles as husband and father evolve. I have found that some challenges will likely never be significantly diminished while others can be, with hard work. You win some and you lose some.

My continuing journey at developing social competence took a quantum leap forward after my wife encouraged me to seek help from a clinician well versed in what is known as Social Thinking®. She learned about Social Thinking from a speech language pathologist and other clinicians who worked with our son, also on the autism spectrum, and she wisely pointed me in this direction after having seen the positive outcomes that my son was able to achieve. Many of the concepts mentioned in this chapter belong to the work of the founder of Social Thinking, Michelle Garcia Winner (access socialthinking.com for more information).

The mission of Social Thinking is to assist people in the development of social competencies so that they may live better lives. It is a methodology that brings structure and logic to the rules that govern social interactions, making them easier to understand. In this regard, Social Thinking has been greatly beneficial to me, because my Asperger's profile favors structure over that which is nebulous and difficult to pin down. My SLP has educated me as to new ways of looking at social interactions, resulting in greater awareness of others as well as enhanced self-awareness. Considering the intensity of my challenges around self-absorption and social unawareness early on in life, my only regret is that Social Thinking did not yet exist when I was growing up. If only I knew then what I know now, though better late than never! At least my son was able to benefit from this amazing organization at an early age.

Learning social competence has been quite a ride, and though I have figured out how to hold realistic expectations of myself and managed to achieve happiness and success, I am by no means resting on my laurels. Much has been accomplished, yet more work remains to be done. How many, if any, of the following social challenges can you relate to?

Self-awareness and social competence go hand in hand:

Growing up, I struggled to connect with others because I was disconnected from myself; in fact, I had no idea just how disconnected I was. I let my obsession with pleasing others and my fear of being disliked dictate how I conducted myself in social situations. I didn't advocate often for my own interests, thinking that doing so would be viewed as selfish. I could not figure out why I had such a difficult time forming substantive friendships given all of my efforts to be likable. This struggle stemmed from my not being aware, until a therapist explained it to me one day, that I was coming off as dishonest toward others because I was not being true to myself. I had been too likable, too eager to please, and therefore less than genuine.

This "eager to please" social strategy was reinforced by my fear of confrontational situations. As long as I did what I was told to do, then I would not get yelled at or be targeted, and all would be well, or so I thought. My mother also taught me that anger is a natural emotion that comes and goes and therefore should not be feared. It took me a long time to learn this lesson. I gradually became accustomed to other people getting angry or frustrated at me, and learned through experience that, though it was uncomfortable, I could survive it. Today, I am thicker-skinned and can better handle whatever might be thrown my way without going into an emotional tailspin. As a result, I am better at being who I am, at saying what is truly on my mind, at being honest with others, and in so doing have become more self-aware. I also find it easier to make friends and function properly in social situations than had been the case earlier in my life.

How do you feel about confrontation? Are you more likely to try to please others so that it can be averted, or would you stand up for what you believe in?

Tuning out:

When I tune out, my mind abruptly and involuntarily goes elsewhere for no good reason. One moment, I am 100 percent focused on what I am doing or what is happening around me, and the next moment I am thinking about something completely different, thereby losing complete awareness of the here and now.

The realist in me tells me that this challenge is probably one of those that can be diminished only to a limited extent. This is because it is difficult for me to improve on a challenge that surfaces when I don't even realize that it has surfaced! Tuning out was a more acute problem when I was younger than it has been in recent years, though it is still more of an issue than I can accept.

The school I attended for middle and high school had a dress code that required me to wear a tie. One day, a classmate of mine decided to pull a friendly practical joke at my expense and tied a knot in my tie (other than the customary knot at the top that sits on the neck). He did so while I was wearing it, and to this day, I have no recollection that this ever happened!

When you take a shower, how often are you left to wonder whether you remembered to shampoo your hair? Or if you used the shampoo without knowing whether it's the first time or the second time? This has happened to me more than once. Do you often catch yourself putting something away only to then take it back out multiple times before you are truly done using it? How often have you driven past your exit off the highway? How about pouring cranberry juice into a bowl of cereal when you meant to grab the milk? I have been guilty of these types of transgressions, repeatedly. When I tune out, I often drive myself crazy, and the list could go on and on, but I'll spare you. I would bet that these mishaps happen more frequently with me than with neurotypical folks my age.

When I fall out of touch with my surroundings, I have no idea that I have done so until I snap out of it myself or unless somebody prompts me to snap out of it. I have learned a couple of strategies for countering this challenge. One is to write down reminders around not tuning out and frequently look at them or repeatedly rehearse in your head mantras like "Stay with it" or "Don't lose touch" or something else along these lines. Of course, you have to remember to use these strategies or they end up being for naught. I find that trying to use them consistently is quite exhausting, and as a result, I frequently end up not using them. Another helpful strategy I have learned is to just not sweat it. Instead, accept it for what it is and sometimes even laugh at yourself. I actually laughed out loud and smiled quite a bit while writing this section.

Social competency and social observation and interpretive skills:

One needs to possess social competency to achieve social observation and interpretive skills, and I am still a work in progress with respect to this—though I am much further along with these skills than I used to be. When I was growing up, I was almost blind to nonverbal communication unless the cue was particularly intense and obvious. Given that, and considering that social communications place considerably more emphasis on *how* something is said versus *what* is said, it was particularly difficult for me to connect with my peers. I would routinely misconstrue what people around me were trying to convey, and I missed out on lots of important information that most others knew. When it came to processing verbal communications, I just about always interpreted spoken words at face value and was not able to understand what "reading between the lines" meant, much less do it.

My difficulties with most modes of communication other than literal, verbal communication had an adverse impact on my efforts at dating and romance. Looking back, I wonder how many nonverbal cues from women went completely over my head. How many women were turned off by my not responding to such cues? How many of them assumed that I was disinterested in them because their body language eluded me and because I did not communicate with them in this fashion? I cannot recall a moment when I looked directly into a woman's eyes, smiled back at her, leaned toward her during a conversation to convey interest in what she was saying, put my hand on her hand, or kissed her with my eyes closed. If I did use these kinds of nonverbal cues while on a date, it would not have been on purpose, and purely coincidental. Instead, I remember plenty of purely verbal communication, lots of shyness, and having to work hard simply to get myself to kiss a woman goodbye. As a result, first and second dates were generally commonplace; I would make it past that point only every once in a while, and even then, nothing significant and reasonably long-lasting would materialize.

Shortly after I began working with the Social Thinking methodology, I found myself in situations to which I could apply social observation and interpretive skills. One day, I stopped at a restaurant for dinner and noticed a stranger sitting several feet away, staring directly at me for a prolonged period of time and more than once, and for no apparent reason. I was able to keep my cool, observe this man's actions discreetly, interpret what I thought they meant, and act accordingly. These were nonhostile, emotionless "blank" stares, and he was sitting perfectly still at his table, so I reached the conclusion that as long as I kept my distance, ate my dinner peacefully, and did not make any eye contact, I would be able to finish my meal and exit the restaurant without incident. While being stared at, I figured that I might have said or done something that bothered this man, though all I had done was walk into the restaurant, wait in line, place my order, and then pay for it. Maybe I reminded him of somebody he once knew and was close to, or maybe he had social skills challenges of his own that influenced his behavior. I will never know, which is certainly fine by me, though thankfully, being able to observe and interpret his facial expressions and body language were sufficient in helping me avoid getting into trouble. I left the restaurant unscathed, feeling proud of myself for handling the situation the way that I did. If this incident had occurred prior to my work with Social Thinking, I probably would have either not noticed this man at all or acknowledged and responded to his conduct toward me in a way that might have gotten me into trouble.

Do you find nonverbal communication challenging? If so, Social Thinking or some other similar methodology may be able to help.

The "tactless syndrome:"

I cringe when I think about some of the thoughtless things I said to people during my relatively "unfiltered" and socially unaware younger years, though I was old enough that I should have known better. Fortunately, this is one challenge that I feel has greatly diminished. I eventually grew up and developed greater control over the words that came out of my mouth.

Earlier in this book, I mentioned a few tactless remarks that I leveled against my own mother, but her knowing me the way she did, she let me off the hook. It simply doesn't work that way with everyday people, and when it came to them, there were consequences. How I spoke to others affected how they thought and spoke of me, sometimes to my face and many times behind my back, I'm sure. Too many cases of abruptly changing the subject in the middle of a conversation. Too many remarks that failed to take the feelings of others around me into consideration. Too much talking about myself without expressing enough interest in the person with whom I was speaking. It all stemmed from a combination of often wanting to be at the center of attention, having a lack of awareness of the other person, and my autism spectrum profile.

In seventh grade, my social studies teacher administered a test in which we had to label several of the fifty states on a map of the USA. Beforehand, he made it perfectly clear that we had to be silent as he announced the name of each state that we were to label. In light of my middle school being located in my hometown of Princeton, New Jersey, when he said "New Jersey," I involuntarily blurted out something along the lines of "You better know the answer to this one." Unsurprisingly, this outburst got me into trouble, and with good reason. I was immediately asked to turn in my map and leave the classroom prior to the conclusion of the test. (Lucky for me, after class was over, my teacher allowed me to complete the test and later gave it back to me with my score and the words "Be careful" written on it.) When I said what I did, it simply did not occur to me that there might have been others in my class who hadn't lived in New Jersey for as long as

I had or who hadn't yet visualized exactly where New Jersey was on a map of the United States. Furthermore, I am not proud of how I disrespected my social studies teacher, whom I liked and greatly admired, and those classmates who may not have known the correct answer.

Many lessons learned the hard way, through experiences like my seventh-grade social studies gaffe, as well as with the Social Thinking methodology, helped me acquire the sense of tact that I now have and wish I had back in the day. A profound statement from the late, great Muhammad Ali says it all, in my opinion. To paraphrase, he stated that during his later years, when he was battling Parkinsonism, that the diagnosis was one of the best things to ever happen to him in that it taught him to talk less about himself, take a step back, and listen to others.

The "social fake:"

The "social fake" strategy can be used to address the "tactless syndrome" challenge. It enables us to behave in ways that are consistent with social norms and helps maintain a state of tranquility. The social fake requires us to pretend that we are in a mood other than the mood we are actually in at the time. It is a routine strategy, even though it requires us to be less than honest with other people. For example, when you are asked, "How are you?" and you respond by saying, "I'm fine, thanks," even though you are feeling anything but fine, you are using the social fake strategy.

Whenever you give a politically correct response to a question or comment that, if responded to honestly, would result in others around you feeling offended, you again are using the social fake strategy. Same story if you say something other than what you are really thinking to a loved one if she is in a fragile mood or if saying exactly what you thought would bring her down more than she already is. Use the social fake only on an as-needed basis, when the hidden rules of the situation warrant that it be used.

Before I knew of the social fake strategy, I often and unintentionally said things that drew sometimes-intense criticism from others (my seventh-grade social studies teacher, for example). I frequently succumbed to "brutal honesty" by impulsively deciding to call it the way I saw it without regard for other people's feelings. Today, not so much, in part because of my use of this strategy.

Understanding social situations and their associated "hidden rules:"

As with several of the other challenges I have described in this chapter, self-unawareness and unawareness of others are responsible for my earlier struggles with breaking the "hidden rules" of social situations, and Social Thinking accounts for why I understand them now.

Every social setting carries unspoken expectations that people have of one another. These expectations determine the hidden rules of the social situation at hand. Before I understood this concept of hidden rules, I would often violate them without being aware that I was doing so. Because of my learning disability, which coexists with my Aspie profile and affects how I perceive the world around me, I tend to process information from social situations differently than most others do, and lots of information tends to escape me. Before I began working with my speech language pathologist and the Social Thinking methodology, I tended to interpret a given situation based only on what I could hear, see, and feel in the moment, and what my senses detected would often be interpreted at face value. As a result, I had either only partial or no awareness of hidden rules and expectations because many or all of these were simply invisible, beyond my realm of perception.

Case in point: the break room at my workplace. The expectations that govern our break room include either expressing an interest in the personal lives or work of other co-workers there, or, if one chooses not to partake in any conversations, quietly listening and avoiding drawing attention to oneself. It used to be that I frequently and unknowingly shirked these expectations. While eating lunch in the break room, I tended to hyperfocus on what I was eating rather than talk to my colleagues, and my eyes would only look in one direction: down, at my lunch. Though I hyperfocused on my food quietly, I can only assume that how I was eating was probably conducive to negative attention, at least from time to time, and that at least some of my co-workers may have thought that my break-room behavior implied disinterest in what was going on around me and in the people around me.

Under these and many other social circumstances, self-absorption is a real killer, not just for me but for many others on the autism spectrum. We unintentionally break the hidden rules without having any idea that we have done so, and people may judge us as a result of this kind of behavior. Therein lies the dilemma of many Aspies: our not meaning to be antisocial yet frequently being criticized, ridiculed, or bullied because we come off that way. I have learned the hard way that intent means little while actions, appearance, and how others perceive and interpret these mean everything!

A little awareness and knowledge make all the difference. Thankfully, I am now more socially competent and therefore more socially aware, far more adept than I used to be at taking stock of a social situation soon after entering into it and remaining engaged throughout its duration. Today, when I walk into the break room, I consciously make a point to listen and either join an existing conversation or initiate a new conversation with one or more of my co-workers. While doing so, I leverage what I know about their projects at work or their lives outside of work and ask them questions about what they are up to.

You cannot lose when you ask constructive questions. By doing so, you are expressing a genuine interest in others while amassing more knowledge about them, which you can use during future social interactions. I think of my knowledge of people who matter to me, which includes my co-workers, as "personal folders." It helps to be able to attribute a tangible concept to valuable information that must be kept organized if it is to be successfully used.

The "social-emotional chain reaction:"

Whenever we do something around other people, they either feel nothing or something, depending on the nature of our action, and then they either leave us alone or treat us accordingly. How they treat us influences how we feel about them and about ourselves. That is the essence of the "social-emotional chain reaction."

Back in high school, when I was essentially living in my own spectrum profile–imposed "sphere of unawareness and self-absorption," my classmates seemed to know many things that I did not. One of these was where a beloved member of the school staff always parked his car. One day, I unknowingly parked my car in his spot, in part because there was no sign telling me that the spot was off-limits, and also because of what I call "tunnel vision," an aspect of my Asperger's profile whereby I notice, to the exclusion of all else, only what I feel I must notice to do what I need to do. Whenever I arrived at school, all I ever felt that I needed to do, and therefore all I ever paid attention to, was to find any open parking spot, get out of my car, and look straight ahead while walking toward the building where my locker was. I tended to function strictly on an as-needed basis. Consequently, I had no knowledge of the hidden rules surrounding the spot that I claimed for myself that day. In my mind, I simply did not have a compelling reason to know; that is, until the social-emotional chain reaction kicked in and a firestorm ensued. Because I was emotionally vulnerable at the time, because I had no knowledge of the social-emotional chain reaction, and because I was unable to anticipate the intensity of other people's emotions as a result of my mistake, I was significantly hurt, so much so that this incident has been permanently seared into my memory cells.

It was obvious to me that several of my classmates were critical of me over what I had done, and one faculty member literally screamed at me at the top of his lungs in front of others. I ended up feeling that my classmates were justified in how they felt, given how loved and respected the person was whose parking spot I unknowingly stole, and so my general opinion of them did not change. However, I ended up feeling intense anger toward the faculty member who harshly singled me out and humiliated me in front of the school community. I thought that he should have handled the situation in a more responsible fashion. Only recently, now that I am pushing fifty, have I been able to fully get past my anger toward him. I also felt ashamed of myself and extremely self-critical. How could I have not known something that probably most folks who drove to school knew? So many strong emotions in me and others as a result of an uninformed decision about a parking spot. Go figure!

I have since been able to forgive the faculty member who yelled at me, realizing that I had it coming. At the time, I couldn't expect the faculty member to know, in the moment, how sensitive I was or that I had "tunnel vision," so all of it is water under the bridge as far as I am concerned. Besides, it's not healthy to hold on to anger for as long as I did. In fact, when I returned to my high school for my twenty-fifth reunion, I ran into him and my feelings toward him were perfectly sound.

Now that I am thicker-skinned and armed with knowledge of the social-emotional chain reaction, I know not to treat an honest mistake or somebody getting angry at me as if it were an epic disaster. This can be challenging, and it requires the understanding that your actions and decisions affect others. You cannot expect someone to respond to you in the way that you would prefer, but you can deal with your own feelings after the fact.

Perspective taking:
For a long time, putting myself in other people's shoes to better understand their points of view was not a priority for me. More than that, doing so simply did not occur to me, mostly because of my "sphere of unawareness and self-absorption." Marriage, fatherhood, and Social Thinking mostly account for why I have been able to address this challenge and begin to truly see other people and respect their perspectives.

I recall an incident during my college years, when one person among a group with whom I was hanging out in our dormitory asked if we all wanted to order a pizza. Naturally, a conversation ensued about what kinds of toppings everybody wanted, at which point I insisted (in *that* kind of tone) on what I wanted, rather than listen to what everybody else preferred. So much for perspective taking! Though I eventually forfeited my preference and said, "OK, sure," to what we ended up settling on, the damage had already been done. My roommate later called me out for it, and I once again succumbed to my still-common tendency to "come around after the fact."

Conversely, when I was eulogizing my mother at her funeral and revealed my autism spectrum diagnosis to provide context for all that she had done to help me, I exercised perspective taking in a way that I had never done before. I made it clear, *before* revealing my diagnosis, that the eulogy was all about my mother, even if it seemed at times to be more about me than her, for this was indeed her day, her funeral. Furthermore, I reached out to those at the funeral whom I knew had autism spectrum profiles or who had family members on the spectrum, saying to them, "If I end up saying anything about what I am about to reveal that makes you feel uncomfortable, I apologize in advance." It was not a coincidence that the "pizza incident" happened before I started a family of my own and before I knew of Social Thinking. What I said at my mother's funeral was anything but coincidental, given that I eulogized her having already become a husband and a father and been immersed in the Social Thinking methodology with my speech language pathologist.

Making predictions and assumptions about people and acting accordingly:
During my student-teaching semester as a music education student, I was invited to a meeting that included some of the most respected and experienced high school music teachers in the region at the time. While there, a question was brought up that I believed I could respond to in a meaningful fashion, despite being the journeyman student teacher among the area's finest in my field of study. And unfortunately, I took the bait! I call this "being pulled toward the stimulus," wherein I can't resist the temptation to respond to something or somebody in the environment, even without awareness

around the likely consequences. Instead of taking stock of who was with me at this meeting, predicting how they would probably respond to my remarks, and refraining from saying anything due to such a prediction, I succumbed to a behavioral tendency associated with my Aspie profile and ended up speaking when I should not have.

Roughly a week or so after the meeting, a fellow student music teacher and I ran into another attendee who was of significant political influence in the local music educators' community. She spoke exclusively to the other student teacher, telling him the great things she had heard about him and about all of the teaching opportunities she had in mind for him once he graduated. She never gave me the time of day—not a word, and, if memory serves, she didn't even make eye contact. Only now am I able to guess why. Clearly, not only did I make the wrong choice in speaking when I should not have, but I did so in front of the last group of people any aspiring music educator would ever want to offend. Looking back on the incident, I now know that I should have remained quiet and been an attentive listener, as would be fitting for a student in the midst of masters.

From what I gather through conversations with people both on the autism spectrum and not, experiencing these social challenges to some degree is common, and I would argue that those of us on the spectrum and those of us who are not have more in common with one another than we might realize. We all have our strengths and our imperfections. That's true of everybody, no exceptions. At the end of the day, we all share a common humanity. We all want to be treated with decency and feel valued for who we are in spite of our imperfections. If more of us can come to understand this and try to refrain from making "us versus them" comparisons, then we become better people and the world becomes a better place!

CHAPTER 3

RISING ABOVE BULLYING

The first time I remember being bullied was thankfully without serious consequence. One day during fifth-grade recess, the world all of a sudden went dark. Then I opened my eyes to find myself on my back, lying on the blacktop, surrounded by a bunch of kids shouting and looking down at me with the perpetrator standing directly over me. I got up and walked away. That's it! I have no recollection of pain, injury, or emotional hardship. There was no trip to the infirmary or the hospital. Life simply went on as normal, as if nothing had happened.

No doubt, there was certainly more to this occurrence beyond what I recall. Perhaps my brain is protecting me from the greater reality by not allowing me to remember the entire story. I will never know what transpired before I blacked out or how I was forced to the ground, and I am more than OK with that.

What I do know is that I was extraordinarily fortunate for having escaped at least mostly intact, if not completely unscathed, given who the bully was and his capacity for intimidation. He was taller and more imposing than me, and he had a reputation for not being nice. He *thought* he was the stronger and smarter one, though in reality, he was neither stronger nor smarter. There is no question that thinking of him in this light helps me ward off any emotional scars.

In that year of fifth grade, I was especially vulnerable to bullying because of my social skills deficits, self-care-related challenges, and personality quirks associated with my autism spectrum profile. These traits set me apart from just about everybody else in my grade. Furthermore, the lone recess supervisor had anything but a commanding, authoritative presence, so there wasn't anybody out there who could realistically protect me. All told, I was a sitting duck, a spectrum kid who didn't know it but was nonetheless expected to mingle with schoolmates just as everybody else did.

In one respect, I am happy that a big deal was not made out of this one incident, because I was spared from being reminded of it and was therefore able to quickly put it behind me. Another part of me feels as though a big deal should have been made, however, because an innocent person got forced to the ground and could have been seriously hurt, both physically and psychologically. When something like this happens out in the open in front of a sizable portion of the student body, a school community–wide dialogue about bullying seems fitting. I have no recollection of any such dialogue. I certainly would have remembered it had it happened.

What does the word "strength" mean to you? When I run an Internet search on the words "bully" and "bullying," I come across definitions that refer to the bully as having superior strength, as dominating others to get them to do what he or she wants, and that refer to the victim as being "smaller" or "weaker." I wonder about that. I define strength as being more than just a physical attribute. It also exists inside, in one's mind, heart, and soul, which I think of as "inner strength." Anybody who needs to bully others to feel strong and whole is not as strong as he or she might appear. I believe that this kind of dependence on a show of force is actually a sign of weakness. I will therefore never accept that I or other victims of bullying are smaller or weaker than their bullies. If you have ever been bullied, as many unfortunately have been, my hope is that you never believe you are weaker than any of the bullies who targeted you. If you have allowed anybody to persuade you into believing this way, it is never too late to believe otherwise!

I encourage you to "rise above bullying," to develop the ability to see the bully for who he or she truly is, to remain true to yourself and not let the bully force you into being somebody you are not, to continue to live your life as you did before the bullying incident, and to not let any bully lead you into a perpetual state of fear or depression. Inner strength enables us to rise above. We deserve better than to feel scared. We deserve to be happy. Otherwise, the bully wins. Don't let the bully win!

In fifth grade and well beyond that year, I had no knowledge of what inner strength was—though in hindsight, I must have had it going for me given how I was able to rise above the bully that day during recess as well as other bullies I encountered later in life. It is remarkable how I was able to leverage inner strength as a survival mechanism despite not even knowing it existed within me. I cannot pin down when I finally arrived at an understanding of my own inner strength—though at least I am aware of it now and can tap into it when I need it most.

One summer's day at sleepaway camp, a bunkmate of mine, whom I recognized as being smart, strong, and generally likable, bullied me by dunking me several times underwater during our free-swim activity. He might not have thought much of it at the time, perhaps viewing it as nothing more than fooling around, but it was certainly a big deal to me (though I didn't come close to drowning). Strangely, I continued to respect and admire him, probably because at that stage of my youth, I did not have the self-respect to know that he did not deserve my admiration after what he had done.

Once summer camp came to a close, my mom and I were discussing how it went. I made a comment that suggested that the bunkmate bully was somehow above me, to which she replied, "Sam, even [bunkmate's name] is no better than you are," or something along these lines. Thankfully, I knew back then that my mom was wise and worth listening to. I took her words to heart and was then able to see this bullying episode for what it was, arrive at a better understanding of who my bunkmate truly was, and move on with another good life lesson under my belt.

Particularly during my formative years, I was a trusting soul, arguably too trusting of people whom I did not know well. I tended to believe just about everything I was told, and in one case, I paid the price. Again at sleepaway camp, a campmate who had evidently figured out how gullible I was led me to believe that an exceptionally beautiful young woman at the camp had a crush on me. I bought what he had said, approached her when I noticed that she wasn't talking to anybody or doing anything, nervously attempted a pickup line that did not stand a chance, and was quickly rejected in no uncertain terms.

Although I do not consider this to be a bullying incident in the literal sense, it might as well have been one in that somebody exploited one of my vulnerabilities with the goal of bringing me down. He could not have predicted that I would walk away from this unscathed, shortly after being turned away, probably assuming that I was sufficiently emotionally fragile to have been scarred by this embarrassment. Looking back, I find it unsettling though typical that I did not know all of this was a setup. To this day, my Aspie profile allows obvious realities to not occur to me, as if there is a blockage in my brain that won't allow them to register. This is less of an issue today than it was that summer. In any event, I celebrate the fact that in this case, inner strength ultimately won out, yet again!

While attending an athletic camp during spring break of my sophomore year of high school, I ended up having to live with a bunch of bullies who intensely teased and ridiculed me and were quick to point out that my athletic skills did not compare to theirs. Instead of focusing on their arrogance and obnoxiousness, I consciously chose to look past them and focus my attention on the roommates with whom I got along well and on the fundamental purpose as to why I was at this camp: to up my game. When I checked in with my mom and informed her as to what was going on, she gave me the choice of either leaving the camp early or staying until the end and fighting through. Thankfully, I chose the latter. I wasn't going to let these bullies derail what I chose to do for spring break that year. Doing so would have let them win. Never let the bully win! Never let anybody or anything get in the way of your plans and goals.

In college, I knew two people in my dormitory who may have bullied me, but then again, maybe not, as strange as that may sound. I am ambivalent about this in that on the one hand, they may have intended to do right by me by trying to open my eyes to how they felt I was coming across to other people and to what they either knew or assumed regarding what other people thought of me. Furthermore, they spoke to me in a calm, relatively quiet tone and were not in any way hostile. On the other hand, they did not ask me, but told me more than once to come with them to their dorm room, knowing that I would follow them every time. Then they would tell me to sit so that they could talk down to me by saying things like "Sam, people are critical" or "People will judge you" or "What are you doing?" as if to suggest that I was some kind of weirdo engaging in aberrant behaviors. These episodes never got physical, unlike the bullying incidents on the fifth-grade playground and during summer camp. And they were not nearly as verbally intense as what I endured at the spring break athletic camp (it seems that when we grow older, the act of bullying becomes more subtle). Nonetheless, they were etched into my memory just the same because of how strange they were and how odd it is to me, looking back, that I voluntarily followed them and let them lecture me.

If I knew then what I know now, I would have either walked away or told them something along the lines of "I don't have time for this" and that would have been that! Regretfully, I didn't have the resolve or self-confidence to leave or just say no, and so I continued to go with them and hear them out, though at least I was strong enough not to let their words sadden or depress me. Once they were done saying what they needed to say, I walked off, took perhaps a few minutes to process what had just happened, and then college life went on.

Bullies need help just as their victims often do. At least some bullies have themselves been bullied or abused earlier in life, and so they end up resorting to bullying to "make things right," to be able to feel strong after having been made to feel weak, or maybe because they did not receive the help they needed after they were bullied. I believe that if a bully seeks help and can eventually come to understand that happiness and fulfillment come from within rather than from exerting power over others, then he or she can be rehabilitated and learn to stop bullying. If you have been the target of a bully, try to understand that there is probably a legitimate explanation for why the bully behaves the way he or she does. I know, not an easy task by any means, and it is not meant to excuse bad behavior or keep you from standing up for yourself. Rather, if you can put yourself in the shoes of the person who victimized you, then you are more likely to rise above any future bullying by virtue of knowing that the person who bullied you is just as human as you are, may have been bullied just as you were, and has probably endured more than his or her share of hardship.

My sense of optimism enables me to extract positivity from adversity. Consequently, my experiences with bullying appear to have helped me grow stronger and wiser, not weaker, as a result of pulling through and emerging intact. In chapter 4, I describe the process of how I learned to love myself as being a long, hard-fought battle during which I grew stronger as I made progress. In this regard, I view self-love, inner strength, and by extension, the ability to rise above bullying, as being inevitably connected in that if you manage to grow in one of these respects, you will also grow in the others at the same time. I also protect myself by knowing to anticipate that others might try to bully me because of some of the same factors that accounted for why I was vulnerable to the fifth-grade bully, including lingering challenges around social awareness and unique personality quirks. And so the question becomes, do we change who we are in trying to avoid being bullied, or do we be who we are and prepare to take a stand if we are targeted? Be who you are, at all costs!

Let's consider bullying from a "big picture" perspective; I find that doing so can be helpful. I view my ability to rise above it as being rooted in my reluctant acceptance of what I have seen arise from the darker side of human nature. As such, I am able to fortify my "inner defense" against any form of adversity that may be headed my way, including any bully with whom I might cross paths. Sadly, we hear too many stories in the mass media about war and oppression, the deep divisions inherent in our politics, a prevalence of "us versus them" tribalism, and bullying and criminal behavior on the part of some who are in positions of power in our society, to name a few. Though I am an optimist at heart, I am also a realist in many respects. While I view the efforts being made to expose and address bullying, divisiveness, and injustice as being worthwhile and inspiring, I know that these societal ills will remain with us, at least to some extent, for the long haul.

I acknowledge that it is relatively easy for me to say what I do about rising above bullying. After all, I have been most fortunate to have had access to a robust support system (my family, friends, clinicians, etc.), I was not bullied as frequently as I know others have been, and none of the bullies who targeted me managed to inflict permanent scars. Are there people in your life to whom you could turn for support, perhaps an immediate or extended family member, friend, teacher, therapist, or significant other? Do you know a bully who has victimized others? If so, it may be worthwhile to seek out those folks so that all of you can cope, heal, and support each other, together. If you have been bullied and are struggling with the fallout, know that my heart goes out to you, that I share in your pain and hope you can rise above it should it happen again. Learning to not let bullies get the best of you often involves hard work and patience. If you repeatedly tell yourself, "I'm done letting bullies keep me down," that's a good start. If you feel that you deserve to attain this goal, believe that you can attain it, invest the time and effort, remain focused, and seek help from others who care about you and are able to help you, then it can be achieved. Otherwise, the bully wins. Don't ever let the bully win!

CHAPTER 4

LEARNING TO LOVE MYSELF

Learning to love myself is one of my greatest accomplishments. I say that because of how long I fought this battle without ever quitting, how much energy I poured into the fight, and because there is no greater gift, and nothing more beautiful, than to love who you are.

I consider my efforts to build self-esteem a battle, because while growing up and well into adulthood, I knew that I was different in several respects from my peers, and it was against this perception of being different that I had to fight to move toward self-love. Prior to college, I did not know that my sense of self-esteem was low because I did not understand what "self-esteem" meant. What I did know was that I was kept back a year in school, whereas most of my classmates were not. I knew that I had a learning disability that warranted my involvement in special education, whereas most others were not learning-disabled and did not require special education. I knew that I talked slower, needed considerably more time than others did to complete certain tasks, reacted slower to what was going on around me, was not "in the know," did not have as many friends as others did, and often stayed home while others were out and about. My inner battle for self-love took place amid these and other realities connected to my autism spectrum profile that held me back, while all that I had going for me was working to move me forward. It was a fight between these opposing forces for the upper hand in determining my self-identity. This is why my road has been a winding one, and why my walk down this road has been long and slow-going.

In hindsight, it seems to me that the first major signs of progress in my inner battle for self-love started to surface during my high school years. It was during this time in my life that I made strides in how I took care of myself, in developing my aptitude for music, in consistently performing well academically, and in becoming involved in a variety of other extracurricular activities. I managed to make the cross-country and tennis teams and compete in both of these sports at a reasonable level, I held a weekend job, and I started having an easier time making friends and growing these friendships. As I achieved musical, academic, athletic, social, and other successes, my self-esteem grew. My aforementioned "sphere of unawareness and self-absorption" persisted through these years, though thankfully it did not interfere with these pursuits to any significant extent.

My sophomore year of college brought a golden opportunity to begin a transformation. It was during this year that my emotional state took enough of a dive to finally force my sphere of unawareness and self-absorption to begin to crack. Not one but a few women in whom I was interested had kept their distance, and my efforts to fit in did not pan out the way I'd hoped, leaving me with nobody whom I could truly call a good friend. I felt isolated from others, including my roommate and those who lived in our section of the dorm. The sweet bliss of not being fully in touch with my greatest vulnerabilities and sensitivities as well as not understanding the true depth of my loneliness all of a sudden gave way to misery when I became acutely aware of all of this all at once. For the first time since starting piano several years prior, I completely lost interest in taking lessons, despite greatly admiring my jazz piano professor. I was one depressed soul that year, though thankfully not clinically depressed such that I needed antidepressant medication. I was not suicidal, just very melancholy.

College presented more difficult social challenges relative to high school. I believe that this is why my "crash" year happened while in college. My middle and high school years were wonderful: I attended a small private school with a strong sense of community, and remarkably a sizable majority of the people across every aspect of that community, not just the student body but also faculty and staff, was likable and easy to get along with. Life was well structured, predictable, and easy to manage as a result. I felt sheltered and secure at a time in my life when I very much needed to feel that way, and I thrived.

Those of us with Aspie profiles tend to function better with structure and predictability, and I am no exception. By contrast, the social landscape I encountered in college was less structured and predictable, and therefore more challenging. My college was significantly larger than my high school. Parties and other social events and gatherings involved larger numbers of people, and the student body included a greater diversity of people, many of whom had backgrounds and life experiences that were unfamiliar to me. As a result, the work involved in connecting with people and cultivating friendships was more complex and sometimes overwhelming. These types of social circumstances are often difficult for those of us on the spectrum to handle, and again, I am no exception. As evidenced by my sophomore-year hardships, the adjustment was not an easy one to make. I needed help, substantive help, to properly adjust.

By the time sophomore year finally wrapped up, my life had come to a crossroads. I could have chosen to do nothing and let myself descend further into the abyss, or I could have looked optimistically at my situation, viewed it as a growth opportunity, and taken action. Thankfully, I chose the latter. I turned to my mother and said to her, in so many words, "Mom, I need help with a few personal issues that emerged this past year. Can you refer me to a local therapist whom you trust and whom I can talk to?" She ended up referring me to a talk therapist with whom I met regularly over the course of a few weeks that summer, and who helped me turn things around. As I recall, we discussed why it was important for me to begin to think more highly of myself, why I needed to be myself around others so that I would come across as genuine and honest, and that it is OK to not satisfy everybody. I was very much a perfectionist back then, often setting the bar too high for myself. In doing so, I was setting myself up for discontentment, which did indeed come crashing down on me that sophomore year. The therapist helped me to open my eyes to the flaws inherent in my perfectionist mind-set, enabling me to begin to free myself from the mess in which I found myself.

As a result of a few sessions with the talk therapist, I finally arrived at an understanding of what self-esteem truly meant. Only then could I start to work on it in earnest and build self-love at a meaningful pace. The progress I had made prior to my work with this clinician was all well and good but ultimately half-baked, because it was made without any awareness of what I was working toward. Becoming aware was transformative in this respect, and the transformation would not have happened had I not "crashed" and then sought help. This is how adversity can become advantageous. Rise up to it and you just might become transformed in the process.

After seeing the therapist, I began to see immediate results with respect to the quality of my collegiate social life and how I felt about myself. My inner battle for self-love had reached a turning point, though the fight was far from over.

To this day, I remain beyond grateful to those people who were in my corner at this critical juncture in my life. I credit my mom not just for being well connected within the community of clinicians and for leveraging that connectivity to help me but also for understanding my desire to seek help from somebody other than her, even though she was an experienced and accomplished talk therapist in her own right. As a result, I was able to work with the therapist to whom she had referred me without feeling any guilt, and I was free to turn to my mom with those matters that I, as her son, felt comfortable bringing up. She ended up saying to me something similar to what my therapist had said, that I had much to be proud of and that I deserved to think highly of myself. Lastly, I credit the talk therapist for being easy to talk to and adept at figuring me out, understanding what I was going through, and finding a way to provide real, useful, and ultimately life-changing advice.

The process of learning to love myself, which began long before my work with this therapist and continued to pick up steam afterward, entailed many small steps taken over a long period of time. As I wrote earlier, it all started with my mother and father and how they chose to raise me, as well as the lessons I learned and efforts I took while growing up. It wasn't until I was twenty-one years old that I finally became aware that my sense of self was compromised in spite of all of my prior work, and it wasn't until sometime in my forties that I finally felt sufficiently strong and self-confident to consider my inner battle for self-love as having been won! Today, I feel as though nothing or nobody can break my spirit or force me to be somebody other than who I am; again, one of my greatest accomplishments. Why did it take so long?

Because I had epic amounts of hard work to do. I had more lessons to learn, more challenges to confront, more times to fall down and find a way to get back up and keep going. I had to be open to advice that was not always easy to hear but that I had to take to heart and use to move myself forward.

Marriage and fatherhood, more than any of my other pursuits, embodied the lion's share of the hard work to be done in earning self-love, as I will explain later on in this book. My work with Social Thinking, as well as career success, and my aptitude for music also helped. In addition, it was beneficial to have friends and acquaintances who were willing to bring to my attention how I was coming off to others in social situations. For example: when I requested a song at a school dance that nobody could dance to and was called out for it; when I was going overboard in repeatedly expressing my feelings about a girl in school who was unavailable and I needed a wake-up call to stop; when I was sitting anything but upright at a dinner table and tuning out during a social event and was told about it afterward. All of it, and then some, fit into the equation. Once I became aware of what was worth working on, only then could I get the work done, and as I worked on myself, I moved closer to my goal.

As an Aspie of fifty years who didn't know it until turning forty, I have experienced more than my share of trials and tribulations, many of which my learning disability could not explain and which I therefore did not understand until I was diagnosed. I have been bullied several times, both physically and verbally. I have heard people say unsavory things about me to my face and behind my back (or so they thought). I have been singled out and embarrassed in front of my peers more than once. I have been cut down to size and been told that I am hated too many times. I have either been stood up or left behind on more than one date and been told "yes" and then "no, I'm sorry" by the same person. In school and at work, I have had to work probably twice or three times as hard as most others to achieve a similar result. I have had to put up with my own haphazard, roundabout ways of doing many things, often getting it right the second or third time instead of the first. I have had to face the consequences of taking too many things personally or at face value. I have often been misunderstood while having only the best of intentions, and I have had to contend with my tendency to be overly hard on myself whenever I do something wrong that is less than criminal. I was even put down by a well-reputed therapist, who, in no subtle terms, said something hurtful about me directly to me without any regard for the vulnerable state I was in when I went to her for help. And yet, today, my sense of self is strong and I am proud of who I am.

While these kinds of struggles are often toxic to self-esteem, the damage they might otherwise inflict can either be mitigated or outright jettisoned by understanding several realities and by using them to develop inner strength and self-love. Have you been through a process of self-esteem building? Have you emerged happier and stronger than before, or are you still struggling? The following realities helped me significantly:

You are unique and special:
There is nobody exactly like you anywhere in the world. This is as it should be, so don't try to be like somebody else. Otherwise, the world is missing out on the real you!

You are not the only one:
Why isolate yourself by thinking that you are the only one with problems, when everybody everywhere confronts challenges and carries emotional baggage? I know that it is easy to fall into this trap when you're feeling down, though you owe it to yourself to fight this tendency.

Accept who you are:
I had a difficult time with self-acceptance while growing up, and I wasn't even aware of this struggle until it dawned on me later that self-love is impossible to achieve without it. In retrospect, I realize that accepting my learning disability during my formative years was simply off the table. Instead, I chose to fight it. Knowing that I was different, I longed to "be like everybody else," and I falsely convinced myself that the grass had to be greener on the other side. As a result, I wanted out of special education and instead to be fully included in the general education classroom, like "everybody else." While in high school, I was offered the opportunity to take the SATs untimed but quickly rejected that option without a second thought because

I was too proud to "take the easy way out," insisting on being evaluated on the same terms as my peers. I was still denying, fighting, and not accepting the reality of my learning disability as being a unique aspect of my identity that entitled me to benefits that I should have used to my advantage. Little did I realize that this fight was probably doing more harm than good. If I could do it all over again, I would have accepted my learning disability as a part of who I was, I would not have been obsessed with distancing myself from special education, and I would have taken the SATs untimed, knowing that doing so would have resulted in me being able to finish the test and earn higher scores.

As with all of my other challenges, self-acceptance took a long time to achieve. After my Asperger's diagnosis was handed down, I had a relatively easy time accepting and ultimately embracing it as being core to my personality despite it being a huge shocker at first. At the time, I was older and wiser, more mature, and had made it further on my journey toward self-love. In this respect, I now have no regrets that I was diagnosed late.

Try, at all costs, to either accept or, better yet, embrace who you are. Otherwise, you are sentencing yourself to a lifetime of unhappiness. If you are on the autism spectrum, or if you are coping with some other disability or disorder that is adversely affecting your sense of self-esteem, work toward either dismissing the words "disability" and "disorder" or learn not to take them at face value or let them get under your skin. It does not help to think of a key aspect of who you are as being a disability or a disorder. The same holds true for the word "diagnosis." Even if a clinician did diagnose you, you do not need to take this word at face value. I find that it helps to think of autism or whatever you are contending with as being a "profile" or as being a unique aspect of your identity. Being able to think in these terms will help you arrive at self-acceptance. As you may have already gathered, I use the words "disability," "disorder," "diagnosis," and "profile" at will, throughout this book, to keep from repeating any one of these words too often, and because these words are commonly used in connection with the autism spectrum and learning challenges. I also do so because I am finally at the point where the "D-words," as I call them, do not get under my skin and compromise my self-esteem.

Figure out who you are and be who you are: These go hand in hand with accepting who you are; all three proved inseparable for me in learning how to love myself: *you* need to define what you believe in, what is important to *you*, and what *you* stand for. Do not let others do so for you.

If you have an autism spectrum profile, don't hide from it or deny it. Instead, either accept your profile and all of its aspects, or work to diminish or conquer some or all of those aspects that *you* feel should be addressed, as *you* see fit. It is often a good idea to listen to other people's advice and criticism, and to ask for these when you need them, as I did—though it is always up to you as to how you use it.

The therapist I saw after my sophomore year of college, and my mother to some degree, helped me see my habit of being too eager to please others. This habit stemmed from my fear of confrontation and of not being liked, fears that many on the autism spectrum feel. (This fear persists in me to this day, though thankfully to a considerably lesser extent.) In continuing to make too many choices based on what I thought others wanted or what others expected of me, I ended up not doing enough of the essential work that I should have been doing in developing a sense of who I truly was. Once my sessions with the therapist wrapped up, I was able to begin the work of self-discovery and developing the courage to be me. In doing so, I found that not everybody who knew me would accept me for who I was, and such people might even judge and criticize me. But I would not let them bring me down. Instead, I stayed strong and didn't compromise myself to please them.

Nobody is able to satisfy everybody, and there is nothing wrong with that. It's a fact of life, and fundamental to human nature. However, you can certainly find the strength to rise above the hostility and negativity that often emerge when something is said or done that dissatisfies or bothers others, or with which others disagree. Finding that kind of strength is not easy, but it can be done. I am living proof of it. I have found that being good to yourself and to others, advocating for your own needs and interests (doing so is not a selfish act), and spending time on activities at which you are proficient and that you enjoy will all help build inner strength.

Avoid "me versus them" thinking:

I have learned not to think in terms of "there's me, and then there's everybody else" or "I am not neurotypical like they are," and instead I think in terms of "We are all human." I use the word "neurotypical" several times throughout this book only because I know it is a word with which many people in the autism spectrum community are familiar and can understand, but in truth, I am critical of this word because I feel that it makes it too easy for people to categorize other people as either "normal" or "not normal" and therefore invites the "me versus everybody else" comparison, which should be avoided if you want to learn to love yourself. Society today is rife with too much divisiveness already, and the victims of divisive ways of thinking often suffer from compromised self-esteem. It is all too prevalent in our politics, and with respect to many personal characteristics (such as race, sexual orientation, religion, age, gender, and on and on the list goes) that should be celebrated for their diversity rather than used as a basis for discrimination. Why add neurotypical versus autistic to the mix? Instead, embrace who you are, embrace "neurodiversity," celebrate what makes you special, and recognize that everybody everywhere is human despite the differences that exist among us.

Discover and cultivate your talents, abilities, and interests:

At a young age, I began to work on my sense of self by spending time developing my aptitude and passion for several pursuits. I did not need to be exceptional at everything, and I benefited simply by engaging in activities that were fun, satisfying, and enlightening. As I discussed earlier, my father was particularly influential when it came to opening doors to pursuits at which he knew I would be proficient, and which would end up positioning me for eventual self-love. He encouraged my involvement in tennis and long-distance running, and he steered my brothers and me toward music by virtue of his and his extended family's long histories with it. Music would eventually become more than one of my talents; it would become core to my self-identity.

My ongoing passion and capacity for academic achievement lifted me up. My father's truly exceptional work ethic and both of my parents' love for their professions were inspirational in this regard. Earning good grades and amassing knowledge made me feel smart and proud, and diverted my attention away from my learning disability. "What learning disability?" I often wondered. I looked forward to every report card, was eager to find out if I made it into the advanced placement classes of my choice, and had a hard time waiting to find out where my class rank and GPA would fall. Thankfully, the desired outcome was there far more often than not. I worked hard for those outcomes.

My Aspie profile has endowed me with abilities that have served me well. Yes, that's correct! Asperger's is not entirely about challenges and adversity. It brings meaningful strengths as well, which can be leveraged to earn success and build self-esteem. For example, as with many folks on the autism spectrum, I am particularly detail-oriented, analytic, and adept at thinking "outside the box." The benefits of these attributes play out in different ways: As a computer consultant, attention to detail is of critical importance as is a capacity for analytic thinking, another common talent among spectrum folks. If a single aspect of a system is overlooked, it could mean the difference between a happy client with a fully functional system and an irate client with a system that underperforms or that might not even be able to be plugged in! If a client turns to us for assistance in solving a problem in their information technology organization, it takes an analytical mind to know the proper questions to ask and what to do with the answers while figuring out the optimal solution to the problem at hand.

As a student, thinking outside the box can bring a subject to life. In twelfth grade, I needed a topic for an American history research project. I envisioned writing about one of my favorite twentieth-century American jazz musicians and including a listening guide to a few of his better-known compositions, thinking outside the box in terms of how I could incorporate my love of music into a history paper. My teacher gave the green light and thought it was one of the best student research papers he had ever read.

Lastly, on a radically different note, it recently dawned on me that the reason the hood on my heavy coat always came undone when it got windy was because the strip of Velcro meant to keep it closed was too thin and therefore not sufficiently adhesive. Rather than make a trip to the dry cleaner only to have them clean the coat, I also knew to ask their tailor to fix the hood by replacing its Velcro strip with a larger, more adhesive strip. That way, I will stay warmer next winter because the part of my hood that covers much of my face will finally stay closed! If this example put you to sleep, I apologize, though it does go to show that I look at something even as mundane as this, which probably would not cross most people's minds, as being a prime example of how I put attention to detail to use.

Remember: a half-full glass of water is always half-full, never half-empty:
I was lucky to have been born an optimist surrounded by many optimistic people throughout my life. I choose to extract positivity and value from frustration and disappointment. I find that if I have had a bad day, I am able to not let it depress me for too long by saying to myself that, in all likelihood, tomorrow and the next day will be better.

I believe that it is possible to choose to become an optimist if you are not already, though it is not as easy as flipping a switch. If you are pursuing a goal and get sidetracked, don't quit. Instead of letting mistakes and adversity get you down and keep you down, look at them as learning experiences that can help you grow and make you stronger. Abraham Lincoln did just that after growing up poor, losing many lower-profile elections, failing in business, and suffering a nervous breakdown. He then went on to become one of the United States' greatest presidents.

Seek help and advice:
I repeatedly drive this point home throughout this book, but still probably not often enough. Don't go it alone if you are having a hard time. Furthermore, do

not think that you are weak-minded just because you need help. Arguably, all of us could use at least a little help from time to time.

Your behaviors toward other people affect your inner sense of self:

When I was younger and more introverted, and less aware, I often acted and spoke without regard for others, and during those years, my inner sense of self was compromised. For quite some time now, my personality has been such that I feel good about myself whenever I reach out to others. My paying-it-forward mission, my work as a computer consultant, and my roles as husband and father are prime examples of personal endeavors that put me in a position to give of myself for the benefit of those who matter to me, and consequently, I have learned how to love myself. How you treat others and how you view yourself are inevitably connected. Use this reality to your advantage.

Be aware of the personalities of the people with whom you associate:

I have had colleagues in the workplace and teachers in school who encouraged me to pursue excellence by setting high standards for me to live up to, and I have benefited from the wisdom and guidance of clinicians who helped me move forward toward self-love. From them I have learned to seek out smart, happy, and successful people, to pursue friendships with folks who were able to see the good in me despite my deficits around social competence. I also learned to distance myself from unkind, ill-intentioned, and chronically angry or depressed people. These types of folks tend to want everybody else to be just like them because that would justify and legitimize their attitudes and behaviors. As a result, they frequently try to bring others down to their level.

It is impossible to completely avoid undesirable people. At school or in the workplace, you must simply learn how to put up with these people without letting them get under your skin. One way to do so is by seeing them for who they are, as having their own personal struggles and challenges, and by having sympathy (without sacrificing your own safety or well-being). Work on cultivating relationships with people who are kind, open-minded, and interesting.

Realistic expectations are essential to self-love: Early on, I was exceptional at beating myself up over mistakes that were not entirely my fault or that were by no means criminal. Self-criticism was but one of several habits that stemmed from me expecting too much of myself. For example, unknowingly parking my car in a highly regarded person's spot, as I discussed in chapter 2; accidentally playing a song on my car stereo, not knowing that it would bring up unpleasant memories for a friend in the passenger's seat; inadvertently asking one of my college professors a question during a strictly lecture class. I obsessed over achieving perfection with respect to my technical abilities as a pianist and my creative abilities as a songwriter. Whenever I had a successful first date with a woman, I often let myself get carried away, envisioning a lasting, substantive relationship with her, expecting to win her over simply by committing myself to growing the relationship. As a result, I would get my hopes up over the prospect of having a girlfriend, overlooking the fact that it was merely a first date and not considering that she may have not felt the same way about me.

I often blew expectations of myself and others out of proportion, and in so doing, set myself up for disappointment and compromised self-esteem. The higher my expectations, the more likely I was to feel let down. One year, the family of a neighborhood friend led me to believe that I could go with them on their family trip. I believed them and expected to join them. The day I knew they were leaving, I got so excited that I ran up the street with a pile of clothes in my arms. I ended up on my hands and knees on the sidewalk, sobbing and in disbelief after realizing that they had already left. I must assume that, somewhere along the line, I had either misunderstood something or took too literally a comment that they had made in jest or not seriously. Maybe I heard what I wanted to hear, rather than what they were actually saying. One of these explanations probably fits. In any event, who was I to expect to go on their family vacation, considering that I was but a friend of one of the family members!

I expected the people I knew to always treat me well because I believed that I always treated them well. I expected others to make time for me whenever I needed their attention, to cater to my sensitivities, to not be critical of me unless I was doing something that *I* felt was wrong, to always take my interests into consideration, to always see value in my best intentions even when my actions did not reflect these intentions, and to tune down their expectations of me because I had a learning disability. I was living in a sphere of unawareness and self-absorption, and my overinflated expectations of others centered around one person: me. And I didn't even know it!

As a result of the gradual forward progress I was making with respect to self-awareness, awareness of others, and self-love, I was eventually able to open my eyes and see how unrealistic my expectations were both of myself and of others, after which I was able to bring them back down to earth. Doing so helped me come to terms with a few realities. Life is often hard and unfair for everybody. Other people have their own problems to deal with and therefore will not always be able to do what I expect of them. When I put myself in other people's shoes, I began to understand them better and take their situations into consideration. Consequently, my expectations of them became more realistic, I became stronger and less dependent on others to feel happy, and I figured out how to adjust the expectations that I held for them and for myself.

Today, I accept and have made peace with behaviors that bothered me earlier in my life and that persist to this day because I do not expect quite as much of myself as I used to. If I make a mistake—like when I'm washing my hands and before I know it, the bar of soap comes loose, falls onto the counter, and then slips into the trash, leaving a mess in its wake—it is no longer the big deal that it used to be. If I am driving along and pass my destination one or more times, or if I look around endlessly for something that ends up having been in my pocket the whole time, I do not beat myself up over it. If I am alone in public and one of my quirky behaviors surfaces, like when I laugh at myself or smile for no apparent reason because I am either daydreaming or thinking about something humorous, I am OK with that, even if it raises eyebrows or results in others looking over at me. When I do something that upsets somebody I care about—like when I inadvertently interrupt my wife, a co-worker, or friend, or neglect to listen properly to what is being said to me—it does bother me, though to a considerably lesser extent than used to be the case. In other words, there is not as much emotional housecleaning to do before my mind calms down. Not all that long ago, it had been commonplace for a firestorm to rage inside of me for a long time over a less-than-earth-shattering mishap.

One more thought regarding high-functioning autism, expectations, and self-esteem: as a high-functioning Aspie, I have tended to come off to most people as being neurotypical when they first meet me or don't know me well, and I'm sure that I am not the only one with a high-functioning spectrum profile for whom this holds true. This reality is problematic for me and others in that it is human nature to form opinions and expectations of somebody soon after the initial encounter, and often people who don't meet the expectations that are placed on them face unfavorable consequences. I was always expected to behave and interact with my peers as if I were neurotypical even though I was not. Therefore, to preserve self-esteem, I have learned to expect that I may be misunderstood, criticized, judged, mocked, and even bullied by others so that I will not be caught off guard or brought down by anybody who treats me this way. In this respect, being able to anticipate what others may expect of me and how they may treat me helps me shape my expectations of them.

Patience is a virtue:
My "inner battle for self-love" has lasted for the better part of my life thus far, past when I got married and became a father, past when I learned of my Asperger's diagnosis, and encompassing all of the work I have done with numerous clinicians and all of the guidance my parents provided, and in the face of ongoing challenges and adversity. If you have been walking for a long time down a winding road as I have, and you are not yet where you want to be, remember that it doesn't all come together overnight. Allow for mistakes and self-forgiveness, and keep going!

If you are less than content, would like to feel better about who you are, and feel that the time is now to make a change, my hope is that you will find at least some of what I have written in this chapter and in this book to be useful to you. Working to build self-esteem was no cakewalk for me, though the time and effort involved were more than worth it. There is no greater gift than to love who you are. If you are ready to embark on this journey, consider the following analogy to the American civil rights movement. Though there is considerably more work to be done with respect to improving race relations in the United States, the civil rights movement did achieve lasting results and positive change in the face of all kinds of odds, and it did so without any help from the Internet or social media, after centuries of slavery and in the midst of Jim Crow–era segregation and discrimination. Furthermore, it required the efforts, struggles, and sacrifices of an immeasurable number of people, a multitude of individual acts of courage, protests and marches, federal government involvement, a timeless letter written from a jail cell, and epic court battles to succeed. The key takeaway? Meaningful change is hard, slow to come, often achieved in the face of adversity, and entails many small steps taken over a long period of time. These are the ingredients of change that allow it to take hold and last, whether in society at large or deep inside oneself. Are you up to the challenge? I hope you are. You deserve it!

CHAPTER 5

MUSIC AND THE WAY FORWARD

All of us, whether neurotypical or on the autism spectrum, face some challenges that are extremely difficult if not impossible to address and other challenges that can be addressed if sufficient time and effort are invested. My Asperger's profile presented a number of challenges, such as establishing and maintaining meaningful friendships, sustaining awareness of my surroundings, and building self-esteem, that were considerably more pronounced while I was growing up than they are today. My ability to manage those challenges was greatly helped by my involvement in music. In my life, its power has been nothing less than transformative.

My first meaningful experience with music was with the violin when I was in fourth grade. It was with this instrument that my performing career began, with my elementary school's string ensemble. Subsequent performing opportunities arose with the trumpet starting in fifth grade, followed by the piano and singing in eighth grade. I went on to perform with orchestras, bands, and choirs of many sizes and styles of music for many years to come. I benefited greatly from all of these group music experiences in that everybody in a given ensemble needs to listen to what is going on around them, feel connected to everybody else, and commit to what the group is collectively doing to deliver a solid performance.

Because of my involvement with these ensembles, my general level of awareness of others around me increased over time. Participation in music groups, as well as summers spent at music and creative arts camps, also provided golden opportunities for making friends in that it was easy to find others who shared the same passion. We rehearsed and performed music together, attended concerts together, listened to music and talked about it together, and visited one another in our practice rooms when we needed breaks or wanted to listen in on what others were practicing. We lived and breathed music together, immersing ourselves in what we loved. A good number of my most lasting and memorable friendships were established in this fashion. Pursuing social activities in which there is a shared purpose or interest can be most helpful in these respects.

Music does not exist merely for the benefit of the listener; it can also be a form of "feel good" therapy for the musicians who make it. Use it or some other meaningful activity as a positive distraction from the banality of everyday life as well as hardship, stress, sadness, frustration, and the gamut of "difficult" emotions. We all need a release from these realities. In music, I discovered a pursuit at which I was able to become sufficiently proficient such that I was granted many memorable performance opportunities that provided welcome departures from the humdrum, day-to-day rhythm of my existence. These performances were not only therapeutic. To me, they represented accomplishments from which I would derive a strong sense of self-pride and that proved to be valuable with respect to my efforts at learning how to love myself. My choir singing took me to Boston's Symphony Hall, where I performed with the Tanglewood Festival Chorus and the Boston Pops Orchestra for their Holiday Pops series. My college choir was invited to perform at Lincoln Center in New York City to rave reviews in the *New Yorker* magazine. I had a solo piano gig at a local Holiday Inn for a few years and was once approached by a woman who enthusiastically told me that one of the songs I played transported her back to a time and place that she fondly remembered and missed. One of my rock 'n' roll bands regularly played at a venue that was always packed to capacity with audiences that stood only inches away from us, feeding off the sound and the energy emanating across the room. The way everybody responded to our band and the chemistry that I could feel flowing through my veins as I took it all in account for what made these performances memorable.

Though it was wonderful to be able to enjoy these and other successes with music, I do not want to give the impression that they were required for music to be beneficial to my work in addressing my Asperger's-related challenges. I still would have benefited had they never occurred. I have derived great contentment simply from spending time playing piano in the living room, in a practice room at music camp or college, or in my bedroom, where I had my keyboards and recording studio set up. I experienced satisfaction as I worked to improve my piano technique, composed new material, or played along with my favorite records blasting over the stereo system. I was at peace with myself whenever I took a walk to the park or sat by the pool with my pen and notebook and wrote song lyrics. Teaching private piano lessons and volunteering to direct a senior citizens' choir were self-esteem boosters in that I took great pride in being able to contribute to the betterment of others.

I did not have to be at the top of my game or become world famous to better myself in the ways that I did with music. All that I needed to do was take the time to enjoy what I loved, work hard enough at it to be able to develop just enough talent to open a few doors, and share my passion with others. Find something that you enjoy, and share it with others. You will likely find that doing so is therapeutic.

During my later high school years, I went through a phase that I would call "girl-crazy." In retrospect, I feel as though entering into this phase was unavoidable in that between school and my weekend job, I met many classy, intelligent, beautiful, kind, and unforgettable young women to whom I couldn't help but be attracted, all at the same time! Plus, I was awash in the hormones that go with being a male teenager. As great as it was to know all of them and to be able to see them on a regular basis, this situation was challenging in that I felt overwhelmed by more emotions than I could effectively regulate at once. For a while, I dealt with all of this by resorting to the extremes of either hiding my feelings or going overboard in how I wore my heart on my sleeve. I look back on this phase as being a perfect storm of teenage hormones, with all kinds of feelings that I could not act on because the women either already had boyfriends or were perceived by me to be "out of my league," and the obsessive tendencies inherent in my Aspie profile, which resulted in me not being able to let go of my feelings despite knowing deep down that moving on would have been best. I had it bad, and yet, I also had it really good, because all of these women were great to know as friends, and I am a better person for having known them.

Eventually, it occurred to me to turn to my songwriting, and using my craft mostly as a coping mechanism, I began to write and record a bunch of mushy love songs for many of these young women. In most cases, I shared the songs with them. Because of the social awareness challenges I had back then, it simply did not occur to me that listening to the songs might have made them feel awkward or uncomfortable, given how expressive the songs were and that we were nothing more than friends. I didn't think twice about giving them recordings of these songs. In one case, I actually played the recording in the presence of the woman for whom it was written, and in front of other people she knew. If I had known then what I know now, I would have never singled her out like that. If memory serves, her body language indicated discomfort as the song played, which today is understandable and regrettable to me. But at the time, I was not able to predict the consequences of my actions. I was hungry for an audience and for the attention I thought the songs would bring my way. And the way I saw it, the songs could only make these women feel good about themselves in that they would be able to hear what they had inspired in me. They told me they were flattered by the songs, and I believed them. Thankfully, my friendships with them were not adversely affected.

The greatest aspect of being a songwriter stems from the freedom I have to write about whatever, or whoever, is on my mind, and I am free to let my imagination take me wherever it will when it comes to how I tell the story. My "girl-crazy" songs are emotionally intense because they reveal how attracted I was to these women while also including plenty of dramatic effect and imagery. While writing the lyrics, I ended up imagining them in various roles. For example, I imagined having a girlfriend who left me, and I would sing about how much I missed and thought about her; I thought about someone I liked not being my girlfriend, and I would sing about how I wished she were my girlfriend and how my love for her kept growing; I reflected on a woman to whom I was attracted and had no choice but to say goodbye to, wondering what might have been and finding it difficult to let go of my feelings. And the reality of it all is that we were just friends. Not what I had hoped for, though in my mind, friendship was, without question, better than nothing.

Expressing myself through these songs ultimately helped me rein in my feelings, cope with them better than I had previously been able to, and come to terms with the reality that I would not be as close to any of these girls as I had wanted to be. It was as if letting my imagination run free and releasing my emotions through music helped me find greater peace of mind and inner strength. Just as with my most memorable musical triumphs, writing, playing, and recording these songs proved to be great therapy for the soul and for my sense of self-esteem, and without needing to be a Grammy-winning piano player/singer-songwriter.

Today, my involvement with music has evolved into something very different from what it used to be. Starting a family inevitably brings about fundamental changes with respect to priorities and how time is spent. I accept that reality, just as I accept the fact that change is inevitable. Family life still involves music, though the time I invest in it is less, and my musical activities revolve around my son. Several years ago when he was around five, I started to teach him piano and music theory, which lasted for roughly one to two years. Afterward, he chose to take a break from the piano and eventually gave percussion a try through his school's band program. Recently, he turned back to the piano and thankfully managed to move past the level at which he was playing when I taught him, thanks largely to what he has learned from his participation in school band as well as my wife's encouragement and guidance. On occasion, the two of us stand side by side at the digital piano we have in our home and play songs in his school music book together. He will start to play of his own volition and then tell me when he is ready for me to join him. He plays one line while I play the other, usually in perfect harmony unless the song requires more practice, and then we switch lines or get creative with the music, playing it in ways other than how it is written. Most importantly, we make playing music together fun, and as a result, we bond nicely while doing so, even if it is for just a few minutes at a time. One thing is for sure: I am no longer the musician of the house, and I am fine with that. In fact, I celebrate it!

My sincere hope for those of you who are not as happy as you would like to be and who haven't yet discovered your passion is that you find it soon, run with it, and do not let anything or anybody get in the way. You will likely end up going through a period of experimentation and trial and error before you land on an activity or a hobby about which you can get excited, but don't quit until you find it, whether it be music, another fine or performing art, reading, creative writing, a sport, an academic subject that sparks your curiosity, et cetera. Hold realistic expectations of yourself in this regard. Not always will a life-enhancing discovery be made overnight.

Back when I was teaching private piano lessons, I had an eighty-year-old student who had never played before I met him. He didn't use his age as an excuse for not jumping into something that might add a little spice to his life, and though the piano ultimately did not work out for him, he earned my admiration for keeping an open mind and putting it to the test despite how old he was. It is never too late to try something new. If you hold on to that attitude, what you end up discovering might transform your life, just as music transformed mine.

CHAPTER 6

CAREER AND WORKPLACE SUCCESS

Many factors, some within and others beyond my control, somehow came together to lead me to success in my career as an information technology consultant. My success story began long before my career was underway, and as with the winding road I have slowly been walking down, this story is not without roadblocks and detours. It all started with my father stressing the importance of hard work and of doing it well. As I mentioned in chapter 1, these values were taught to me by example, as I observed how hard my father worked as a doctor, how passionate he was about his chosen profession, and how adept he was at it. My mother's passion for social work was equally inspirational. Thankfully, there were no defined or lofty expectations when it came to my level of achievement in school, no discussions along the lines of "You must earn straight As, or else." Rather, I was told that my grades would always be satisfactory to my parents as long as I worked hard and tried my best. Because they set reasonable and realistic expectations in this regard, I was able to enjoy learning and appreciate the value of a strong work ethic during my formative years. These same attitudes benefit me to this day.

Once I was in college, it came as no surprise to me or my parents that I decided to major in music within the first few months of my freshman year, given my long-standing passion for the subject. I eventually discovered that people who choose musicology for their livelihood tend to write scholarly books, pursue teaching positions in higher education, or become music critics. I decided that these pursuits were not suitable for me, so I ended up graduating with no career goals and an uncertain future, only to go straight back to school, this time to give music education a try.

I mistakenly assumed that I would do well as a music teacher by virtue of having enjoyed a recent summer teaching job at an arts institute. To make a long story short, teaching music in public school is not a job you can be sure of after merely a single summer of limited teaching within the relatively sheltered confines of a private five-week sleepaway arts camp. Furthermore, it requires nothing less than a strong, unwavering love for teaching in and of itself and for wanting what is best for the students. I discovered during my student-teaching semester that I simply did not have that kind of love for school teaching that I did for music, so I graduated yet again with no defined career path and a teaching certificate that I would never use.

That was six years of higher education without the outcome I was hoping for, though these years were hardly for naught. I received an exceptional liberal arts education that opened my eyes to a universe of knowledge, and that helped shape the person I am today and how I look at the world around me. Having not yet discovered a career path, I remained hopeful and persistent, knowing deep down that I would eventually find one. I also knew that I was adhering to what I had learned from my parents: only pursue a career about which I would feel passionate. Back to the drawing board!

So began a thankfully short-lived period in my life during which I moved from one unappealing dead-end job to another, hoping that something meaningful would eventually surface. I decided to teach piano lessons so that I could put my work in music education to some use. Thankfully, I took much better to private teaching than I did to teaching in a classroom setting. That aspect of my spectrum profile, whereby group situations are considerably more challenging to manage than small group or one-on-one situations, certainly explains why this was so. In any event, private piano teaching was never anything more than a secondary pursuit in that I did not want it to become my full-time profession. A small group of students was more than sufficient for me, and it helped me keep my sanity as I transitioned from one lackluster job to the next.

I do not look back with regret at the temporary, less-than-career-worthy jobs I held after the conclusion of my higher education years and prior to landing my present-day career as an information technology consultant. My positive outlook on life and capacity to learn from my experiences allow me to acknowledge how they helped me grow. Jobs that I held in retail, as a dishwasher, perfume salesman, and customer support representative, were not ones that I looked forward to or that were rewarding enough to become careers, though they taught me what it was like to be expected to work hard in a less-than-desirable work environment. They strengthened me, made me more patient than I otherwise would be, and gave me insight into the types of work and workplace environments that I should avoid. I learned several valuable lessons:

Be wary of the personalities of the people with whom you are working:

In other words, surround yourself with good, hard-working, successful people who take pride in what they do. The importance of this dawned on me while working for a company at which such people were absent! The manager of this company contradicted himself one day when he admitted to me, verbatim, that he would hire "anybody who can breathe" when too many of my co-workers saw their sales numbers suffer and then chose to leave the company. All the while, he had been saying to the new hires how important it was to be working with motivated, successful people, and that "these are the kinds of people you'll work with here." He would also lie about people who resigned, saying instead that "they went on vacation."

I knew I had the wrong job when it became apparent to me that the boss was less than honest in trying to cover up inconvenient truths and more folks were headed out the door than should have been the case. Not surprisingly, the fate of my departed former co-workers soon became my fate and my ex-boss became my vision of the kind of person whom I should try to avoid in the workplace going forward.

If your goal is to settle into a long-term career that will bring you happiness and prosperity, it is not enough to merely enjoy and be proud of the work you are doing. Also understand that the people with whom you work will either make you or break you.

Do not let a layoff adversely affect your sense of self:

Some jobs simply are not meant to last, and that is nobody's fault. With respect to my one- to two-month job in retail sales, the boss was blunt with me, saying that I did what he asked me to do but that he could no longer afford to keep me on the payroll. This was a well-established musical instrument store at which sales slowed down not long after I started, and being the newest employee there, I was the one to be let go. I did not do anything wrong. My timing was a little off, that's all.

If and when you are laid off from a job, try not to take it personally or let it adversely affect your self-esteem. Sometimes things like this happen that are beyond our control and that have nothing to do with something we did.

If you find yourself constantly wanting to know what time it is, do not plan on staying at that job for too long:
This was the case when I worked as a dishwasher at a country club, and when I was a little shy of one year into my customer support job. In both cases, I eventually became too bored to stay, so I resigned, but before doing so, I had my next job lined up. There is nothing worse than arriving at work and repeatedly wondering when you will finally be able to go home. If you find yourself watching the clock too often or checking your smartphone every few minutes, then it is probably time to consider moving on.

Don't waste time and effort selling a product that you do not truly believe in or in which your heart is not invested:
I learned this lesson while selling imitations of popular name-brand perfumes and colognes in outdoor parking lots. Success with this kind of work requires a particular type of personality, which ended up not being mine—though at least the weather was nice while I gave it a try! I followed the script for the sales pitch and managed to sell a reasonable number of bottles, though not nearly enough to be able to afford to keep this job. I jumped in without thinking once about what I would be selling and without investigating how I would be selling it (impulsiveness, a significant challenge that stems from my Aspie profile), and figured I would see where the job might take me. In retrospect, I did not go far because parking lots proved to be a considerably less-than-ideal setting for sales success,

and I could not accept selling merely an approximation of "the real thing." I denied this reality and did not last long on the job as a result.

You will know, deep down, if you do or do not believe in the product you are selling or the service you are performing. Other people will know as well. Listen to your gut instinct. Life is too short for you to be spending your time on something that is less than rewarding.

Don't refrain from pursuing a "stretch" job:
A good job is one that challenges you, and in which you can learn and grow. A friend of mine happened to get her foot in the door at a technology company, and then she recommended that I interview there too. I took her advice despite possessing little of the knowledge I thought I would need to be hired there, though they ended up giving me a chance after I was able to convince them that I was intelligent and motivated enough to succeed at the job. I was told that I needed to pass three training exams to be permanently hired as a technical support representative. I ended up failing the first exam but was not let go because I did not fail by much. I then convinced them to keep me aboard after working many overtime hours to learn what I needed to learn, by passionately telling them how much I wanted the job, and by easily passing both of the remaining exams.

As I have mentioned several times in this book, my Aspie profile is such that I tend to take what others say to me at face value more often than I should, though I know better now than I used to. In this case, I discovered the flaw in this kind of thinking when management proved that they were willing to be flexible with me. When they told me that I needed to pass three training exams to be hired, I took that literally. I was pleasantly surprised to learn otherwise after I failed the first training exam yet kept my job. Their accommodation ended up being the difference between me getting my career started and ending up who knows where. Unlike that lying ex-boss, the folks in the management team at this company were smart, friendly, and honest people who saw enough potential in me to justify giving me a second chance. Second chances like this are not easy to come by, so take them seriously if and when they are granted to you. Because of my second chance, I was motivated to learn more about computers, the Internet, and customer service from a one-month training program and a year on the call center floor than I could have ever anticipated, and I was well on my way.

After that year of providing over-the-phone technical support, I concluded that working with technology in this fashion was not suitable for me as a long-term pursuit. At that point, I moved on to the information technology services company with which I continue to work to this day as a consultant—twenty-three years and counting. When I first started looking for work and a career path, I could never have imagined remaining in one place for this long—though now that I have done so, I am not surprised that it all panned out this way.

So can you tell if a job might be long-term? Here are several factors that create longevity in the workplace:

The work is engaging:
Unlike other jobs I have had, I am not repeatedly looking at the clock all day, wondering when I get to go home. Over the past twenty-three years, my job title and responsibilities have evolved, as has the information technology with which my consulting work is associated. Furthermore, the technology is exciting to work with in terms of its features, capabilities, and the problems it can solve for our clients. For all of these reasons, the work never gets old.

The work is meaningful:
In my job a good number of the technology solutions we design and sell help our higher education, government, health-care and research computing clients make substantive, positive differences in the quality of people's lives and in society as a whole. I am most proud of an archival system I designed for a university library, not because selling it made me wealthy or because the system involves the greatest technologies ever to be invented, but because it enables the long-term preservation and accessibility of video testimonials of Holocaust survivors. Do you feel that there is value in what you are doing?

My colleagues are likable, intelligent, and hard-working people who are passionate about what they do. Do any of your colleagues reflect these work-place attitudes and behaviors?:
In my experience, it takes a team of folks with these characteristics to be successful. Thankfully, my management team developed an exceptional aptitude for recruiting the right people for the positions that needed to be filled to grow the company, filling vacancies as others moved on, and creating and maintaining a culture of effective teamwork. When I joined in 1996, there were fewer than ten of us. Today, we are roughly eighty strong and counting. A good number of us have been with the company for ten, fifteen, and twenty-plus years. This kind of growth and loyalty are not possible without a workplace culture that is conducive to success. Even if we sold the greatest information technology product that ever existed, we would not be successful without the right people to sell it. Thankfully, this has not been a concern.

My work is consistent and predictable—a great asset for somebody on the autism spectrum:
Staying with the same company under the same senior management for more than twenty years certainly provides consistency and predictability. I get to come to work every day knowing what to expect and having established a level of familiarity with my responsibilities, something that brings great peace of mind. These benefits are significant for someone with an Asperger's profile, which tends to thrive under these circumstances.

Prolonged success is an excellent self-esteem booster:
In the "inner battle for self-love" (chapter 4), success plays an important part. I have been greatly helped by my career experiences. Giving of myself to others has always lifted me up, and in my career, I am in a position to not only do so for my clients but also for my colleagues, thanks to our culture of teamwork. Is your current workplace conducive to success? To the enhancement of self-esteem?

There are opportunities not just for professional but also personal growth:
Learning to collaborate with others is but one example of what this might look like for someone on the autism spectrum. I tend to gravitate toward operating on my own terms, and so it took me a long time to embrace the power of teamwork. Thanks to encouragement from management, to being called out more than once for "working in a vacuum," and to my workplace's team-oriented culture, I was eventually able to break out of my shell and become a team player. Consequently, I became less self-absorbed and more aware of others than I had been during my earlier years with the company.

Considering the challenges and adversity I have faced outside of work, I feel fortunate to have had an abundance of career success over the years. As a result, I have much to share regarding the types of workplace behaviors that I have learned to adopt and that have contributed to my success. If you are open to advice along these lines, my hope is that at least some of what follows proves to be beneficial to you with respect to your own employment situation. Please note, however, that if your line of work differs significantly from the work (team-oriented sales and consulting) I have done over the past twenty-plus years, some of my tips may not be relevant to you. With that being said, I frequently use words like "notice," "be aware," "learn," "consider," and "understand," all of which are actions that are universal to all workplace environments.

WHEN YOU ARE NEW TO THE JOB . . .

- Admit it! If you do so, others are more likely to hold realistic expectations of you and be patient with you if and when you make a mistake.
- Understand that all people, to varying extents, are critical, even if they don't come across as being so. Therefore, accept constructive criticism and follow through on that criticism by showing that you have learned your lesson when the next opportunity to do so comes along.
- Do not expect to be respected and trusted as soon as you walk into a new job. Respect and trust must be earned. Being social, being likable, being a team player, and working hard will eventually result in your co-workers respecting and trusting you, though it may take some time.
- As soon as you feel comfortable with your responsibilities at work and with the day-to-day work routine, stop saying that you are new to the job.

Co-workers will not tolerate you playing the "I'm new" card forever.
- Do not stop saying to yourself, "I will be persistent and I will succeed."

BE SOCIAL

- Say "hello" and "How are you?" to your co-workers on a regular basis, and say these things with sincerity. *How* you say things matters significantly more than *what* you say. True, these phrases are clichés, but then again, they are clichés because they are always said and are therefore widely accepted.
- When somebody asks you how you are, say "I'm fine," "Doing fine," or something along these lines, even if you are not doing fine. Only with a close friend, significant other, or family member with whom you work should you be honest with respect to negative feelings. Reference the "social fake" strategy in chapter 2.
- If there is a break room, a cafeteria, or some other gathering place, eat your lunch and take breaks there, rather than at your desk. Do not isolate yourself. Make an effort to be among your co-workers.
- Do not initiate conversations that involve politics or religion. Most folks agree that these two subjects should not be brought up in the workplace.
- When you are having a conversation with a co-worker, lean toward him or her, stay still, and

maintain good eye contact. These gestures show that you are actively listening.

- Be aware of your co-workers' body language suggesting that a conversation should wrap up. For example, loss of eye contact, turning away, crossing the arms, and other visible indications of boredom or impatience.
- People are drawn to other people who look happy, so smile when you are around your co-workers, even if you are not necessarily in a happy mood. Don't be ashamed of faking it in the workplace!

BE LIKABLE

- Treat your co-workers the way you would want them to treat you.
- Ask your co-workers questions that invite them to talk about themselves and others whom they are close to. People love to talk about themselves and what matters most to them. For example: "How was your [weekend, vacation]?" or "What does your [husband, wife] do?" or "What do you enjoy doing outside of work?"
- Learn what you can about your co-workers by listening to them speak to others and by asking them questions, then put what you have learned into a "personal file" for each of them. As you grow the personal files over time, you will have more to talk about with your co-workers.
- Be aware of how busy your co-workers are. If a co-worker is intensely focused on a task, refrain

from saying anything to her. Doing so will distract her from what she is working on, and people do not like being sidetracked, even for a split second. Instead, talk to co-workers during their lunch breaks, when you run into them in the hallway, or when it is obvious that they are not absorbed in their work.

- There are lots of simple, easy things that you can say or do every day in the workplace that will go a long way in your efforts to be likable. A few examples:

  » Say "Thank you" to your co-workers after they say or do something that warrants it. A heartfelt "Thank you" means much more than a quick "Thanks."

  » Say "Bless you" every time somebody sneezes.

  » Hold the door open for people who are about to pass through.

  » Stop/hold the elevator for a co-worker wanting to get on.

  » Bring appealing food in to share with co-workers every once in a while (a dish that you cooked, cookies, chocolate, etc.).

  » From time to time, send an article to a co-worker that you think he or she will appreciate.

  » When you notice a co-worker having a hard time with something, offer to help.

- Work hard! Hard work doesn't guarantee that your co-workers will like you, though being lazy and slacking off on your responsibilities will adversely affect your likability if others notice, and co-workers will notice.

BE A TEAM PLAYER

- Thank your co-workers for their efforts toward shared goals, and let them know that you appreciate and value them. A simple "Thank you," "Great idea," "I am grateful for all you have done," or something else along these lines will more than suffice. If you show your appreciation, they are more likely to thank you and show their appreciation for the work that you do. Studies have shown that people perform better in the workplace and are happier there when they are treated in this fashion.
- Resist the temptation to be a one-man or one-woman operation. Doing so can be particularly challenging for folks on the autism spectrum, many of whom prefer to work alone as opposed to in a team context. If this preference pertains to you, do not hesitate to let your management team know that you may need assistance in learning how to be an effective team player.
- Offer to help your team members, or ask them if they would like help. When collaborating with co-workers as a team, think about what you can do to make their jobs easier.
- Prioritize team goals. The team is less likely to succeed if all of its members are not unified around a common objective or set of objectives.

- Learn your co-workers' strengths and preferences. Be aware of these when you ask them to do something so that they feel good about themselves and look good to their co-workers when they do what you asked them to do.
- Have your co-workers' backs. If a team member is traveling, on vacation, or is all of a sudden dealing with an emergency situation, pick up the slack. Doing so shows your commitment to the team's success and shows that you genuinely care about your colleagues. Nothing matters more than standing up and delivering when the team needs somebody to step up.
- Listen as well as talk. Try to balance the two. Listening to others with whom you work closely shows that you care about what they have to say. Listening becomes particularly important when working closely with colleagues who have more experience and longevity at the workplace than you.
- Consider how your co-workers prefer to communicate. Some folks prefer e-mail, largely because it doesn't demand an immediate response, allowing them to respond to you in their own time and in their own way. Others prefer a phone conversation or face-to-face interactions over e-mail because these modes of communication are more personal and often lead to meaningful outcomes faster in comparison to e-mailing back and forth.
- Be flexible. In other words, learn to step outside your comfort zone when effective collaboration with co-workers demands that you do so.

Stepping outside your comfort zone often entails supporting your co-workers' ideas even when you don't agree with them.

- Resist the temptation to self-promote. Think and speak in terms of "we" or "us" rather than "I" or "me." For example, say "We made it happen" instead of "I made it happen" to other co-workers, even when you are referring to a team accomplishment to which you contributed the most or which you alone initiated.

LOOK FOR WAYS TO COMPENSATE FOR YOUR CHALLENGES

- First, you must figure out what your challenges are, then come up with a strategy for managing them. For example, over the years, I have found that I move slower than most when it comes to completing a given task or project. I am able to compensate for this challenge by often working past business hours or on weekends to meet project deadlines. I also know that I have auditory processing–related challenges whereby I struggle to keep up with all of the details that are said to me during a conversation, particularly if the conversation involves folks who talk fast. I compensate for this challenge by e-mailing my clients or co-workers lists of questions requesting all of the information I require to properly complete a project. I can also use e-mail to verify information

I thought I heard correctly during a conversation but of which I'm not 100 percent sure.

- Don't be afraid to admit your challenges to your co-workers. If they are aware of these, they are more likely to set their expectations of you accordingly and are more likely to give you leeway when you need it than would otherwise be the case.
- Ask for help. Everybody makes mistakes, and if you are new to the job, you are more likely to make mistakes as a result of not yet being acclimated to the workplace. Don't beat yourself up emotionally over such mistakes. Instead, turn to those colleagues who are more experienced for assistance.

USE METHODS FOR ALLEVIATING STRESS

- The occasional deep breath can work wonders in terms of letting go of built-up stress. When you exhale, imagine that all of the stress in your body floats away with your breath.
- Take regular breaks away from your desk or wherever you do your work. If necessary, schedule these breaks so that they become routine and are therefore not forgotten.
- Take a walk. If the weather is nice, walk outside. Otherwise, take a stroll around the office and say hi to your co-workers along the way.

- If it isn't against the rules, listen to music while working, though keep the volume down so that you and others around you aren't distracted.

WORK HARD AND WORK SMART

- Success in the workplace depends more on being social, being likable, and being a team player than on anything else, though this does not mean that you can get away with slacking off on your work when you are strong in these other areas. I have found that these interpersonal skills and hard work are all of critical importance to success.
- Working hard and working smart involve the following: meeting all deadlines, being on time for all meetings and conference calls, following through on all commitments and promises that are made to customers and to co-workers, bringing intelligence and thoughtfulness to the fulfillment of tasks, attention to detail, and taking pride in pursuing excellence (as opposed to barely getting the job done while meeting the minimum requirements or expectations).
- Persistence is critically important. Do not be so quick to quit when the going gets tough. Hang in there as you contend with the challenges that the workplace will likely bring your way. When mistakes are made, try to learn from them and work to put things right. You will become stronger and

more adept at what you do as a result of persisting in these ways.

IF YOU WORK WITH SOMEBODY YOU DO NOT LIKE OR WHO APPEARS TO NOT LIKE YOU . . .

- Accept it, deal with it, and rise above it! You might also find that the other person has a change of heart, perhaps after you prove yourself on a task or project, to give one example. Likewise, you might have a change of heart. Folks can change others' thoughts about them by changing their own behaviors.
- Stay strong, focus on your work, and do your best to treat the person the way you would want to be treated despite how he or she is treating you. Be the bigger person!
- Understand that nobody can satisfy everybody. As hard as I have worked at being likable and showing my clients that I care about the success of their projects, I have had some who asked to no longer work with me. For example, historically, I have tended to talk slowly and have had a capacity for long-windedness. Some of my clients who are fast-paced and who want conversations and projects to progress more rapidly may understandably not be comfortable with my style and request to work with somebody else. I know better than to take this personally. Instead, I focus on those clients to whom I can be of value.

- Understand that some people might distance themselves from you until they have become more familiar with you. As a result, they may *appear* to dislike you when this is actually not the case. They may warm up to you later.

When I decided to write this book, it was with the intent that those who read it would be able to use it to carve out better lives for themselves. The intent behind this particular chapter is no different. You deserve to be engaged in work that you can look forward to when you wake up each morning, work that you enjoy and find fulfilling, at which you can be successful. Whether you do or do not have the privilege of this kind of career outlook, which I am fortunate to possess, I sincerely hope that the ideas shared in this chapter will result in a more satisfactory work situation for you. My fingers are crossed.

CHAPTER 7

FAMILY CHALLENGES AND TRIUMPHS

Family, to me, is an intricate construct. Though I care deeply about my wife and my son, I find managing my relationships with them to be a challenging and complex endeavor because of certain aspects of my Asperger's profile. Contending with the "getting on the same page" challenge has been well worth the effort, considering what I have today compared to when I was single, as well as the degree to which I have grown and how much I have learned as a result of having a family of my own. The experience has been nothing less than transformative in this respect. After almost nineteen years of marriage and eleven years of parenthood, I continue to adapt as I work to address the challenges these roles present, and in all likelihood, I will never be done adapting. The metaphorical road along which I slowly walk continues to wind.

When my wife and I first met, which happened spontaneously at a singles party, we saw little besides the best in each other. The excitement of having her in my life was so strong that I had no interest in dating other women. Looking back, I got away with many "Aspie-esque" social blunders during these early days—behaviors that I would typically expect to result in friction or frustration did not. Once, I said to my then-girlfriend, "Sorry, I'm not available to get together tomorrow because I have bills to pay," after which she calmly convinced me to do otherwise. There was lots of long-windedness on my part during phone conversations, and graceful, quiet patience on her part. After accidentally calling her by the name of the woman I was dating before I met her, she responded, "Be careful." Nothing more, and again she spoke in a calm tone. It is remarkable to me when I remember these and other statements I made that were without consequence but which could have been consequential.

Predictably, and naturally, as time went by and I got to know her better, I gradually started to notice her sensitivities, vulnerabilities, and other personal attributes that were not initially visible to me during the euphoric state early on in our relationship. Likewise, she began to notice plenty about me. It did not take long for her to discover aspects of my undiagnosed Asperger's profile, which we both knew would prove to be challenging to our relationship going forward. I opened up about my learning disability and my challenges around dating and relationships, and she opened up to me about her challenges.

We bonded primarily over our mutual interest in the performing arts. Our first date was a dinner concert at a folk music club. She was an accomplished dance teacher, dancer, and choreographer, and being that I was playing piano and writing songs, she choreographed one of them and we performed it together at her dance studio's year-end recital. I will never forget our rehearsals together in preparation for this performance. It took lots of hard work to make sure the dancing and the music were synchronized, but we pulled it off. We supported each other, not only when we performed together but also by attending each other's individual performances. I fondly remember all of our ballet and musical theater outings. My favorite memory is when I performed the love song I had written for her at our wedding while she was sitting by my side, in front of all of our guests.

After noticing how I interacted with others, as well as how we interacted with each other, my wife wondered if I was dealing with more than just a learning disability. Her curiosity eventually turned out to be prophetic, though it took a while for me to listen to her instincts and begin to investigate the possibility of something else. Prior to our son's birth, I was reluctant to pursue further self-discovery, largely because the knowledge of my learning disability was enough baggage to carry around. Many years prior, I bought into my mother's words of advice that I come to terms with the fact that there would always be challenges associated with my learning disability that I would not be able to fully conquer. Those words stuck, and I figured I would leave it at that. Then my son was born, and as is often said, that changes everything, including my willingness to dig deeper with respect to what my wife felt was worth researching. And as I previously mentioned, I met with a local therapist who ended up recommending a neuropsychological evaluation that ultimately led to the conclusion that I had an Asperger's profile. That diagnosis has unexpectedly brought nothing but good into my life: a more complete picture of who I am, enhanced self-awareness and awareness of others as a result of my work with the Social Thinking methodology and other clinicians, an opportunity to make a difference through my work with the Asperger/Autism Network, this book, and whatever else lies ahead.

As for my son and me, we share a unique bond in that we both have autism spectrum profiles. It is profound to me to see him deal with a few of my early challenges and to see other challenges that are unique to him, just as I had challenges that were unique to the younger version of me. It is also profound, and heartening, to see him do better in areas with which I struggled when I was his age. No two people on the spectrum share the same profile, including fathers and their sons. Considering my passion for music, it is great to see him do as well as he has with the piano, and wonderful that we are able to use music as a way of bonding with each other. We also bond over sports, particularly baseball, just as my father and I did. Thankfully, he won't have to wait until age forty, as I did, to learn the complete truth about his profile, and as a result, he has been able to benefit from early interventions that were simply not available to me when I was his age.

When each of us was born, my son and I were both dealt a hand that we are playing as best we can. After many years of hard work on myself, I have managed to come to accept who I am and have accepted that Asperger's is a part of my identity. My son, eleven years old at the time of this writing, has known for some time that autism is a part of who he is, and he accepts this reality. Since having been diagnosed a little shy of two years old, I have seen him grow taller and smarter, be out on the ocean on a surfboard, perform with his school band, and hit the ball and run the bases at full speed. I have seen him make large strides, either greatly diminishing or conquering earlier challenges while continually contending with new challenges as he gets older. My wife's substantial and unwavering efforts at helping him move forward have been essential to his development. This aspect of her approach to parenting is what I admire most about her.

My greatest hope for my son is that he will continue to accept the autistic aspect of his personality as he faces the challenges that lie ahead. As I wrote earlier, self-acceptance is key to developing self-love, and in my experience, only then can one find true happiness. I am able to anticipate at least some of the challenges he will face as he grows older and what he will need to do to successfully address them, considering that his path will probably be similar to mine in light of the commonalities between our profiles. I can only hope that he will listen to his mother and father and take our advice to heart as we try to help him along his journey.

I have learned, among other lessons, that having realistic expectations is critical for being a good father. Had I not learned to bring my expectations of my son and myself down to earth, I would be a basket case and he might be as well. If I expect too much of him, I set myself up for disappointment and I set him up for failure and feelings of inadequacy, thereby compromising his sense of self-esteem. If I expect too much of myself, then I start to feel overwhelmed and depressed. Instead, I choose to expect that learning lessons and personal growth happen in small, incremental steps over long periods of time. I do my best to pick my battles and bite my tongue when I feel it is warranted. I expect that certain tasks will be performed incorrectly, maybe many times over, before they are performed with success. I expect occasional regressions when a goal is being pursued because sometimes we need to take one or more steps back before we are ready to move forward. I tailor my expectations along these lines because they reflect my life experiences as an Aspie, they take into consideration that my son is also on the spectrum, and they leave ample room for me to be pleasantly surprised when an outcome turns out better than I had initially expected. What a great feeling it is when that happens!

I have trained myself to look at what to others would be relatively incidental steps forward as being monumental achievements for my son. Doing so is a means of maintaining happiness while engaged in the hard work of being an Aspie dad. Given my son's spectrum profile and my own challenges around social awareness when I was younger, I tend to disproportionately celebrate the "little" things he proactively does that show awareness of others around him. He will often lay a blanket over my wife while she is relaxing on the couch without being asked to do so. He will see me approaching our front door and open it for me before I get there, without being asked. "Would you like some of my leftover Chinese food, maybe for dinner tonight?" he graciously offered me just the other day. He frequently approaches me to give me a hug rather than wait for me to hug him, and he often calls for "group hugs" involving the three of us.

I will never forget the day a few years back when my son and I were grocery shopping together at a crowded supermarket. When we first got there, I reminded him, only once, not to push the cart too fast and to keep his eyes wide open for other people around him so that he wouldn't run into them as we moved up and down and between the aisles. Later on, he said to me, of his own volition, "Daddy, we need to slow down and get out of the way—there are other people coming toward us," after which he did exactly that. Probably not many people would think this kind of occurrence worthy of becoming a long-term memory, given that these words have likely been said by many people many times over in congested venues and that this was just another random day at a supermarket. And yet, to me, it was extraordinary. So, too, is the relationship between my son and his dad!

My lion's share of hard work in marriage and fatherhood has been directed toward addressing the many challenges I have confronted and continue to confront in these roles. I have found that there is no way around doing this work if my family is to be a happy one. It is the least I can do considering that my wife and son both have challenges that they are doing their best to address for the betterment of our family. For those of you who are married, parents, or both, with which of the following challenges can you identify?

The ability to understand better courses of action and to put that understanding to work when the time is right are two different things:
The journeys of marriage and parenthood demand that I grow as a person along the way. Over the years, I have learned a great deal from my wife and my son as to how I can be a better husband and father. The challenge for me, by virtue of my Asperger's profile, does not lie in my ability to understand better ways of being a husband and a father, but instead in my ability to break away from yesterday's habits and put these newer learnings to work when it matters most. When impulsivity kicks in, I am unable to think before I act and what I hope to do dawns on me after the fact. As a result, my actions are not always consistent with my intent.

Considering all of the possible courses of action in a given situation, particularly with respect to parenting, the gap that exists between understanding what is best and doing what is best "in the moment" can be daunting for me. For example, I often end up telling my son to do something without enough authority in my voice, even though I know, all too well, the importance of how something is said. Or I may unintentionally be too demanding of my son at times when I should not be, like toward the end of an exhausting or unusually stressful day for him, even though I understand the importance of taking context and circumstance into account. I have found that repeatedly rehearsing my knowledge of "the right thing to do when this happens" in my head can help toward acting in accordance with my understanding the next time around. This strategy is effective only if I am able to keep at it for meaningful lengths of time, which can be taxing.

I know that I am not alone in acting differently than planned or desired. If you struggle with aligning your behavior and intent, I share your frustration!

Tuning out and the possible fallout:
Becoming disconnected, out of the blue, from what is going on around me is unfortunately one of those aspects of my spectrum profile that I will most likely never be able to fully conquer. More sleep and less stress help to mitigate this challenge, but these cannot always be managed. When I tune out while interacting with my family, there is more at stake than when I do so in the presence of others. My wife understandably does not feel acknowledged or listened to. My son is now old enough to be able to detect, on occasion, when I misconstrue what he has said to me during a conversation, and he has already called me out more than once for this. It happens because I sometimes tune out in the middle of talking with him. After he calls me out, I say to him something along the lines of "I'm sorry, I misunderstood you, what again did you say?"

Usually the second time is a charm. Then we're OK. The last thing I want to have happen is for my son to grow older with the perception that his father doesn't listen to him, so I can only hope that my second effort after the initial disconnect is sufficient in warding off that perception.

The only suggestions I can make if you are contending with this is to practice telling yourself repeatedly to remain connected to what is going on around you and to apologize as soon as you become aware that you have tuned out.

Getting "stuck" on opinions:
Just the other day, my wife had to repeat herself five times to get through to me as to a better way to solve a particular problem. She managed to do so without raising her voice, for which I was grateful, and I apologized afterward. The strange thing is, I knew all along that she was correct, yet I nonetheless felt a compulsion to stick with my own approach to the problem. I eventually came around, though the outcome is different from when I validate her ideas the first time. After five go-arounds, she was understandably frustrated. The moral of this story: try to avoid unwavering adherence to your own opinions and keep an open mind.

Gravitating toward defensiveness:
For me, as with many on the spectrum, defensiveness is a coping mechanism that I resort to when I feel like I am being blamed for no good reason or when I am misunderstood. When I get defensive, it is an impulsive, involuntary reaction over which I have only some

control at best. It is a habit I am not proud of, largely because my wife is justifiably sensitive to it. In a way, I am caught between a rock and a hard place when it comes to defensiveness because when I am able to hold it back, I am silent, and during an argument, neither silence nor defensiveness helps. My goal with respect to this challenge is to find that elusive happy medium between silence and defensiveness while in the thick of an argument. If you tend to get defensive and want to do something about it, perhaps my goal can become your goal as well. Just keep in mind that implementing the goal is easier said than done.

Fixating on sensitivities and needs and ignoring those of others:
All of us have sensitivities and needs. My Aspie profile is such that I often forget that my wife has them just as I do. As a result, I am prone to being fixated on my own sensitivities at the expense of hers. Acting defensively, as I explain directly above, is but one example of this challenge. Interrupting her during a conversation is another. In both cases, I am catering to my own need to be heard in a way that violates her need to be listened to. I look at each substantive conversation during which I manage to not cut her off, not talk over her, and not act defensive when I am tempted to do so as a triumph. How often do you put the needs of others you care about ahead of yours, and vice versa?

The emotional expressions of others are not always about me:

I function best in the midst of structure, predictability, and logic. And so it helps if I am able to attribute some sense of structure to that which is unstructured in life, for example, social interactions and human emotion. Doing so is not always a winning strategy, particularly when it comes to how I process what my wife and son communicate to me. It took a relatively long time for me to realize that I cannot expect communications within my family to always be structured, literal, and predictable. Arriving at this realization is, to me, yet another triumph.

I have found that communications that are infused with lots of emotion are rarely conducive to literal interpretation. For example, with respect to anger and frustration, I eventually learned from my wife that it is important to understand where her anger comes from when it *appears* that she is angry only at me, and before I blame myself. If, in this case, I take all her verbal and nonverbal expressions of anger at face value, then I would always feel that I am at fault. Early on in our marriage, when I did not know any better, I usually fell into this trap, and doing so was not helpful with respect to my efforts at building self-esteem. Today, I am more likely to realize that anger can stem from a combination of factors, among them too much stress, not enough sleep, hunger, too much work at the expense of fun and leisure time, those aspects of our existence that cause anxiety, et cetera. I am also better at differentiating between when my wife *seems* to be angry with me but might not be and when she actually *is* angry with me—though making this distinction remains challenging. If I know deep down that I have done something wrong or that I have said or done something that got under my wife's skin in the past, then I am likely to process my wife's anger at me at face value. Conversely, if my wife appears to be angry or frustrated with me at the end of a long, stressful day, and I feel as though I have not done anything wrong, I will most likely not process my wife's emotions at face value. Before you engage in self-blame when somebody gets angry with you, stop, take a deep breath, and think it through.

Contending with the "bachelor state of mind:" And by the way, if you are a woman reading this, feel free to substitute "bachelorette" for "bachelor."

Just as my "inner battle for self-love" involved the tug-of-war between all that I had going for me and the challenging aspects of my autism spectrum disorder, I look at marriage and parenthood as also involving a tug-of-war. In this case, the tug-of-war is between that part of me that wants to do right by my wife and son, and what I think of as the "bachelor state of mind." The latter often feels like a gravitational force inside of me that tries to pull me toward ideologies and habits that I formed when I was single and only responsible for myself. Though I am more adept than I had been at keeping the bachelor state of mind at bay, I still unintentionally gravitate to it mostly because I was in this state of mind for the better part of my life, and because of my Aspie profile.

I entered into my relationship with my wife without any prior long-term relationship experience, mostly because of lingering challenges around social competence. Only two previous romantic relationships come to mind, and both of these were only half-baked. One of them was no more than an "on again, off again" summer-camp fling, in that we reconnected when camp began and went our separate ways when camp ended, over the course of three summers. The other girlfriend, with whom a mutual friend set me up, lasted maybe four weeks, two of which were at a distance once we returned to our respective colleges after winter break wrapped up. I theorize that my "bachelor state of mind" challenge is therefore connected to the fact that until my wife and I considered ourselves a couple, I did not have any sense of what it truly meant to be committed to somebody else.

And so, when I make a decision that disproportionately benefits me over my family, I have lost to the bachelor state of mind, in part because, as a bachelor, I did not need to take care of or worry about a child or a spouse. For example, when I lie down on the couch because I am tired and then I don't move when my son asks me to play with him, I succumb to the bachelor state of mind because opportunities to play with him are relatively few and far between. When I manage to drag myself off the couch in spite of how tired I am, that, to me, is a triumph.

While a bachelor, not all but most of the decisions I made centered around one person: me! Oftentimes, I only needed to listen to a single voice: the voice inside. Not long ago, I fell ill with the flu and stayed home to focus on getting better. When the day came and I felt 100 percent for the first time since getting sick, I told my wife, "I am all better, not a single symptom, so I'm going to work today." She replied by saying, "You might think that you are all better, but you are not. This virus tends to drop off and then come right back. You'll be coughing all over again later today, so you better stay home." Trusting her instincts, which are spot-on far more often than not, I said to her, "OK, I won't fight you on this—I'll stay home," which I did. And, lo and behold, my cough returned a few hours later. Yes! The bachelor state of mind loses out. Another triumph!

Central to my "bachelor state of mind" challenge is the reality that unlearning habits I developed in the past is extraordinarily and sometimes frustratingly difficult. This is true among many of us on the autism spectrum. It explains why the progress I have made on the types of challenges I write about in this chapter and throughout this book has happened slowly and in small, incremental steps, and it explains why some of my challenges may never be significantly diminished, much less conquered. I have often heard women talk metaphorically about their significant other as being "a little boy in a man's body." I must admit that in some respects, this is true of me. I do not beat myself up over it. I have come to accept it. The bachelor state of mind is directly relevant.

For those of you who have had to contend with the bachelor state of mind and wish to do something about it, first try to train yourself to become aware of when you are about to resort to it. "In the moment" awareness is not easy to achieve, but it can and has been done. You might find, as I have, that mentally rehearsing what the bachelor state of mind means, repeatedly in your head, is an effective training strategy. Once you have attained this level of awareness, then you can work at keeping yourself from getting caught in its trap. Lastly, be sure to praise yourself when you succeed at resisting the temptation. Look at these successes as triumphs.

Facing confrontation:
Conflict is unavoidable in any marriage. Consistent with advice my mom gave me about relationships, it is important to not let conflict go unresolved. But fear of confrontation is an attribute of my Aspie profile that made conflict resolution particularly difficult earlier in my marriage. Instead of engaging my wife in a conversation aimed at resolving a conflict, I preferred to avoid such discussions or would resort only to defending myself. Instead of giving her my undivided attention when she tried to explain what she felt brought about the conflict and what could resolve it, I didn't listen because I had a hard time keeping my heightened emotional state from flooding my brain with noise. Furthermore, I would often adopt the "I'm done, let's just forget about it" attitude, which never did us any good.

Thankfully, as time went on, I grew emotionally stronger as a result of gradually becoming more accustomed to conflict situations arising in my marriage. Today, I am more adept at keeping my emotions under control when conflict occurs. I am less likely to get defensive or to walk away in the middle of a conflict situation and more likely to apologize when I know that I am at fault. I still have a ways to go in this department in that I still succumb to defending myself and to not saying sorry when I should, though these happen less frequently than had been the case earlier. How do you deal with conflict? Do you find that it is too difficult to face? If so, I understand how you feel all too well—though dealing with it effectively is essential to the success of any long-term relationship.

Coping with not being on the same page:
My marital union is referred to as a "neurodiverse" marriage in the sense that I am on the autism spectrum and my wife is not. Add to that the differences between us that are gender related and those that stem from contrasting sets of life experiences, and it becomes apparent how much room there is in our relationship for disunity and disagreement. Furthermore, "agreeing to disagree" is not always realistic and is easier said than done.

The frustration that I sometimes feel in connection with this challenge stems from the reality that I often misconstrue my wife's intent when we are talking to each other. I end up thinking that I am correct in my understanding of what she means, only to find that she needs to clarify what she originally meant after the fact. I know that I am listening to her, though she does not feel listened to when I misunderstand her. These misunderstandings are sometimes due to the roundabout way in which I process information.

Case in point: The other day, she asked me to bring my son's "baseball stuff" upstairs. As I see it, "baseball stuff" could imply a few things: his Little League uniform, the equipment bag with his bat and glove, his batting helmet, his baseball card collection, et cetera. Instead of asking her what she meant by "baseball stuff," which simply did not occur to me to ask, I randomly assumed that she wanted his equipment bag, and so that's what I brought up. She then needed to correct me by clarifying that she actually wanted his Little League uniform, not the equipment bag, so that's what I grabbed for her the second time around. Not the same as getting it right the first time.

In this case, initial specificity as to exactly what my wife needed would have averted the confusion. When I do not have a clear understanding of what is being said or asked of me, it is up to me to ask for clarification, though I did not do so in this instance. During a conversation, and not just those that I have with my wife, I am sometimes left to guess what the other person means and then I inexplicably "hit a wall" that keeps me from asking for the information I need to understand and respond appropriately. Instead, I "wing it" and hope that my response is relevant. Sometimes I am on target and other times I'm not. This is but one example of the haphazard way in which I might process information during unstructured social interactions.

When it comes to disagreement mitigation, my approach is to leverage the "Yes, dear" strategy as often as I am able to for the sake of marital unity and tranquility. However, I have also found that there are boundaries associated with this strategy, particularly considering the strength of my beliefs and convictions and my tendency to adhere to my own ways of doing things. As a result, I am not always in a position to say "Yes, dear" or "OK" to her, and disunity ensues. Parental discipline is a good example. We sometimes differ in our approaches to this. A situation that, in my wife's eyes, would warrant disciplining our son may not be discipline-worthy in my opinion, and vice versa.

In another example, earlier in our marriage, I tended to firmly stand by my frugal attitudes when it came to how we spent our money, so much so that I often made decisions that only took into account how much something cost in the short term. By contrast, my wife has always looked at the big picture with respect to making investment decisions. Because of my stance, I was not always able to say "Yes, dear." In the spirit of wanting us on the same page on this matter, I have since learned to be more flexible when it comes to our finances, so this is not as much a point of contention as it used to be. Another triumph!

If you are contending with the "getting on the same page" challenge in the relationships that matter most to you, my best advice is to let your significant other know that you are doing your best to understand and cooperate, and to appeal to him or her to agree to disagree when getting on the same page is too difficult to achieve.

All of the work I have done in addressing these and other marital and parental challenges has transformed me in more ways than one. I am emotionally stronger, smarter, less self-absorbed, more aware of my surroundings, and more patient than at any time prior to my marriage. I have also found that I am more flexible and thoughtful in the way that I live my life than ever before. That's because marriage and parenthood have demanded that I be flexible and thoughtful in these roles.

Though I am doing better with these challenges, I am still not where I want to be, and I may never be. And so these are small steps forward, yet they propel me down this winding road. As I see it, never being fully satisfied with where you are in terms of your efforts at self-improvement is core to being a good parent and spouse. It keeps you growing in the right direction.

CHAPTER 8

LOOKING AHEAD

When I look to the future, I do so with mixed feelings. The optimist in me sees reasons to be hopeful that the road ahead will work out fine, although the realist in me has reason to be concerned. I do my best to do right by my family with the hope that my efforts will result in a brighter future for us. I continue with my paying-it-forward mission, hoping that by sharing my ideas and insights as to how I earned success and happiness, I will be contributing to "the greater good" and to a brighter future for at least some of those whom I am able to reach. I also try to take notice of what goes on around me, in social media, in the news, and everywhere I go. I celebrate some of what I see, although much of it gives me pause.

My father once said to me, “I will never stop worrying about you and your brothers,” even though we were grown adults and out on our own at the time. I questioned why he felt this way, given our ages and how well we were doing. Somehow I thought that a parent is supposed to stop worrying about his sons once they reach a certain point in their lives. What did I know? Only once I became a father was I able to truly understand where he was coming from. Today, I can’t stop worrying about my son, and true to my father’s experience, I cannot imagine ever stopping. I worry because I love him and because I cannot be sure that everything that I want for him will pan out.

And so, when I look ahead to the future, my thoughts can’t help but revolve around my son. I imagine his destiny as the interplay between how he addresses his unique personal challenges as somebody on the autism spectrum and a variety of societal and global trends that will affect him and his generation. I am keeping my fingers crossed that the interventions and therapies that are in place to help him, as well as his parents’ love and guidance, will result in him having an easier time making friends, establishing intimate relationships, and building self-esteem than I had while growing up.

The reality that the unemployment rate in the United States is significantly higher for those with disabilities weighs on me, especially with respect to my son’s career prospects. Though I view the autism spectrum as not being a spectrum of disabilities, I worry about this aspect of the unemployment rate because I know that there are many who do consider spectrum folks as being disabled. I therefore champion those with "distinct profiles" who are working hard on their careers and succeeding. I celebrate those employers who recognize the value of a diverse workforce, see the untapped talent and potential in people with spectrum profiles and give them opportunities to contribute and thrive by having introduced autism-specific recruiting, training, and hiring initiatives. Dell Technologies, Bank of America, Microsoft, Walgreens, Capital One, AMC Theatres, Procter & Gamble, and many others are among them. I am grateful for all of the organizations, including the Asperger/Autism Network and Social Thinking, that devote their efforts to the advancement of those of us who possess alternative neurologies. All of the above give me reason to be hopeful about my son's future in spite of what the unemployment numbers indicate.

Now is a good time to begin to accept neurodiversity as a significant and meaningful aspect of our social fabric. We acknowledge diversity with respect to race, ethnicity, religion, nationality, sexual orientation, skin color, and political affiliation, among others. Why not neurology? Why not view folks like me, my son, and countless others whose brains are wired a little differently as people with unique abilities and challenges, rather than as people with a disability or a disorder? Many who are on the autism spectrum are kind, hardworking, smart, talented people who have made and continue to make meaningful contributions to society. And those who are and are not on the spectrum have more in common with one another than most people realize.

It is clear that autism awareness has progressed a great deal since the 1940s, when the term was first used to describe children with emotional and social difficulties. However, awareness and *acceptance* on a societal level are two different things. The reality is that more people of all ages continue to be diagnosed with autism spectrum and ADHD profiles at increasingly higher rates over recent years. Folks on the spectrum work many of the same jobs as those not on the spectrum. Many are successful doctors, attorneys, chief executives of corporations, fine and performing artists, celebrities, Nobel Prize recipients, and so forth. I am far from being the only Aspie who is college-educated, married, and a parent. Those on the spectrum who are considered to be "nonverbal" may not speak with their mouths, though many of them can express themselves fluently as writers, and some of them are bestselling authors. There has been significant speculation that many famous historical figures had Asperger's profiles, including Albert Einstein, Abraham Lincoln, Benjamin Franklin, Thomas Jefferson, Thomas Edison, Marilyn Monroe, Isaac Newton, Beethoven, and Mozart, to name just a few. Though these are not definitive conclusions, it nonetheless holds true that such speculation happens for a reason. What is known about these individuals' personalities and how they conducted themselves coincides with how many of us Aspies function, and autism has become a more mainstream diagnosis than used to be the case.

This all suggests that it is time for society to accept neurodiversity. If we are able to move toward such acceptance with less discrimination, scorn, and bullying and more cooperation, then understanding and peaceful coexistence could happen. Consequently, I would feel better than I do today about my son's outlook, just as I would feel better about the world in which we all live.

I become uneasy when I consider that my son is growing up in a society that arguably has become characterized by increasing divisiveness, tribalism, prejudice, and hostility between folks of differing political opinions, belief systems, and backgrounds. I, too, find myself getting caught up in the social media and the news climate of "us versus them," sometimes even feeling intense anger toward those who forward an agenda with which I do not agree. This is not who I am, or who I want to be. Naturally, as a father, I'd like to be able to shelter my son from all of this toxicity and adversity, though realistically I know that I can only shelter him to some extent. This reality weighs on me, considering what I know about his spectrum profile, with his sensitivities, vulnerabilities, and anxieties. As I see it, the best way my wife and I can protect him is to endeavor to teach him what my parents and my own life experiences have taught me. It is important to be good to other people because you tend to get what you give in this life. Take a stand for what you believe in, but do so cautiously and thoughtfully so as to minimize the possibility of getting into trouble. Listen to all points of view, all sides of an issue or story, even if you do not agree with some or all of them. It is impossible to satisfy everybody or for everybody to like you, so expect that you may run into people who try to compromise you or bring you down. When and if this occurs, you can rise above it, standing tall. And most importantly, love who you are!

Thankfully, everything that I find troubling fails to reduce my vision of the future to that of Armageddon. That's because I make it a priority to acknowledge the good and the beauty that I see in people and to allow those aspects of us to renew my faith in humanity when so much seems broken. I resist the tendency to look at everything that is going on around me from a one-sided point of view, choosing instead to embrace the bigger picture. These are valuable life lessons for my son as he proceeds down his road. He will understand when he is older.

On a fairly regular basis, I see a woman who works at a supermarket at which I often shop. She is deaf and has some challenges with speech, and what is truly remarkable about her is that neither of these personal attributes holds her back at all. She is as adept and hardworking at her job as all of the other folks who do the same job during other shifts. She consistently acknowledges and smiles at me when she sees me. She happily interacts with plenty of others, and often without the use of sign language. In her own special way, she is as outgoing and friendly as anybody else I know, and those around her respond to her accordingly by smiling back at her. She merely operates a little differently than those who can hear, resorting more to nonverbal communication and less to spoken words in order to be who she is and connect with people. It is wonderful to see, and it shines a light on the beauty of acceptance and inclusivity.

Just as this woman proves how meaningful an honest smile can be, so, too, did a girl who looked to be around my son's age and whom I saw at the same supermarket. She was happily lending a hand to her sister, and her smile spoke volumes to me. It was radiant, obviously genuine, and lasted from start to finish as she helped her sister, who was wheelchair-bound, get properly situated at a table prior to having something to eat. It was uplifting to see a young person be as happy as she was to assist somebody else, considering that she could very well have viewed her actions as being nothing more than fulfilling an obligation. If a critical mass of children can learn what this girl appears to have already learned, that it is important not just to aid others in need but also to take pride in doing so, the outlook for my son and his generation looks promising.

On Thanksgiving Day in 2018, a friend recruited me to volunteer with her at a local soup kitchen. As great as it felt to be reaching out to the hungry and homeless, that feeling paled in comparison to how awestruck I was when I heard how difficult it is simply to secure an opportunity to volunteer at the kitchen. My friend asked one of the folks who manages the kitchen about when she should call in so that she would be one of the first to be considered for a volunteer position for Christmas Day that year. Even then, she could not be sure that she would be able to offer her services. Oftentimes, she called the instant the kitchen was scheduled to start fielding calls from would-be volunteers, only to be repeatedly greeted by a busy signal. After hearing this, I thought to myself,

"If only goodwill of this magnitude could assume a life of its own, take flight, and extend itself to where it is needed the most." Goodwill toward our planet. Goodwill between differently minded people, enabling them to say no to hostility, to agree to disagree, to reach out and compromise, or to at least learn to peacefully coexist. Goodwill that keeps a would-be bully from targeting someone or that levels the playing field for those who currently play according to different sets of rules. Yes, I admit that I am engaging in utopian wishful thinking, but wouldn't it be nice? This is the kind of world in which my son proceeds with his life, though only in my dreams.

And so, my long walk down this winding road continues, into the unknown. I can't know where it will lead because there is only so much I can control. Much of what has happened in my life was unexpected and could not have been predicted. I always knew that I wanted to be married and to be a father, though I had no way of knowing whether I could make it all happen, given my long-standing social competency and self-esteem challenges. None of the many clinicians with whom I worked prior to my neuropsychological evaluation saw my Asperger's diagnosis coming, nor did my mother, my wife, or me. It simply came out of nowhere. Yet today, I am a husband and a dad whose self-esteem is perfectly intact.

English Composition was far from my favorite subject in grade school, and as a musician, I envisioned myself only writing songs. Yet here is this book. Go figure. So onward I walk, at peace with the fact that I do not know what lies ahead, because I could never have foreseen where I am today, nor could I have known how I would end up making my way here. I will continue my paying-it-forward mission, remembering and honoring my parents' legacy, hoping that my efforts make a substantive difference for the better, all while watching my son grow up, worried, and at the same time, optimistic. Onward, and hopefully upward, I go . . .

ACKNOWLEDGMENTS

Just about all of the people I wish to thank are written about in these chapters. Your names are intentionally not mentioned in this book because of my decision to respect your privacy, except for those of you who warrant acknowledgment because of my use of terms and ideas that are attributable to you. To all of you, words cannot express the depth of gratitude that I feel for you for making a positive difference in my life.

As for all of the clinicians I have been privileged to meet over the past few years at the Clinical Training Level 1A Social Thinking Boston training sessions, I am not half the writer I am today and this book is not half of what it has turned out to be had it not been for the honest feedback and opinions you shared about earlier versions of these chapters as well as my blogs. I feel spoiled to have been the recipient of truly invaluable editorial critiques on a monthly basis from so many of you. As such, my appreciation for you knows no bounds.

ABOUT THE AUTHOR

© 2019 Nikki Cole

Sam Farmer wears many hats, among these, father, husband, musician, computer consultant, and autism spectrum community contributor. A resident of Massachusetts, he writes blogs, records coaching videos, and presents at conferences for the Asperger/Autism Network, sharing what he has learned with the intent of helping others help themselves. *A Long Walk Down a Winding Road* is his first book.

Made in the USA
Middletown, DE
02 November 2019